Arabesque

This page & opposite
Freya, by Marie Wallin, *pattern page 26*

Previous page
Blyth, by Marie Wallin, *pattern page 36*
& Brogan, by Marie Wallin, *pattern page 44*

This page
Rhiannon,
by Marie Wallin, *pattern page 37*
& Phoebe,
by Marie Wallin, *pattern page 28*

Opposite
Phoebe

This page
Jocelyn, by Marie Wallin, *pattern page 47*

Opposite
Sebastian, by Marie Wallin, *pattern page 24*

This page
Reuben,
by Martin Storey, *pattern page 38*

Opposite
Holly, by Marie Wallin,
pattern page 34

This page & opposite
Lillith, by Marie Wallin, *pattern page 45*

This page
Seth,
by Marie Wallin, *pattern page 42*

Opposite
Kaitlin,
by Marie Wallin, *pattern page 30*

This page
Larissa, by Marie Wallin, *pattern page 49*

Opposite
Fallon, by Marie Wallin, *pattern page 48*

19

Opposite
Grace,
by Martin Storey,
pattern page 32

20

SIZING GUIDE

When you knit and wear a Rowan design we want you to look and feel fabulous. This all starts with the size and fit of the design you choose. To help you to achieve a great knitting experience we have looked at the sizing of our womens and menswear patterns. This has resulted in the introduction of our new sizing guide which includes the following exciting features:

Our sizing now conforms to standard clothing sizes. Therefore if you buy a standard size 12 in clothing, then our size 12 or Medium patterns will fit you perfectly.

We have extended the size range of our patterns, with over half of the designs shown being available to knit from size 8 to 22, or Small through to Xlarge.

The menswear designs are now available to knit in menswear sizes Small through to XXlarge ie. 40" to 48" chest.

Dimensions in the charts below are body measurements, not garment dimensions, therefore please refer to the measuring guide to help you to determine which is the best size for you to knit.

STANDARD SIZING GUIDE FOR WOMEN

UK SIZE	8	10	12	14	16	18	20	22	
USA Size	6	8	10	12	14	16	18	20	
EUR Size	34	36	38	40	42	44	46	48	
To fit bust	32	34	36	38	40	42	44	46	inches
	82	87	92	97	102	107	112	117	cm
To fit waist	24	26	28	30	32	34	36	38	inches
	61	66	71	76	81	86	91	96	cm
To fit hips	34	36	38	40	42	44	46	48	inches
	87	92	97	102	107	112	117	122	cm

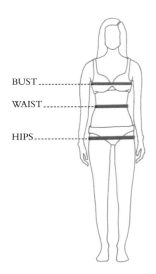

CASUAL SIZING GUIDE FOR WOMEN

As there are some designs that are intended to fit more generously, we have introduced our casual sizing guide. The designs that fall into this group can be recognised by the size range: Small, Medium, Large & Xlarge. Each of these sizes cover two sizes from the standard sizing guide, ie. Size S will fit sizes 8/10, size M will fit sizes 12/14 and so on.

The sizing within this chart is also based on the larger size within the range, ie. M will be based on size 14.

UK SIZE	S	M	L	XL	
DUAL SIZE	8/10	12/14	16/18	20/22	
To fit bust	32 – 34	36 – 38	40 – 42	44 – 46	inches
	82 – 87	92 – 97	102 – 107	112 – 117	cm
To fit waist	24 – 26	28 – 30	32 – 34	36 – 38	inches
	61 – 66	71 – 76	81 – 86	91 – 96	cm
To fit hips	34 – 36	38 – 40	42 – 44	46 – 48	inches
	87 – 92	97 – 102	107 – 112	117 – 122	cm

STANDARD SIZING GUIDE FOR MEN

UK SIZE	S	M	L	XL	XXL	
EUR Size	50	52	54	56	58	
To fit chest	40	42	44	46	48	inches
	102	107	112	117	122	cm
To fit waist	32	34	36	38	40	inches
	81	86	91	96	101	cm

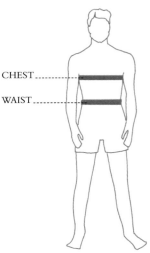

MEASURING GUIDE

For maximum comfort and to ensure the correct fit when choosing a size to knit, please follow the tips below when checking your size.
Measure yourself close to your body, over your underwear and don't pull the tape measure too tight!
Bust/chest – measure around the fullest part of the bust/chest and across the shoulder blades.
Waist – measure around the natural waistline, just above the hip bone.
Hips – measure around the fullest part of the bottom. If you don't wish to measure yourself, note the size of

a favourite jumper that you like the fit of. Our sizes are now comparable to the clothing sizes from the major high street retailers, so if your favourite jumper is a size Medium or size 12, then our casual size Medium and standard size 12 should be approximately the same fit. To be extra sure, measure your favourite jumper and then compare these measurements with the Rowan size diagram given at the end of the individual instructions.
Finally, once you have decided which size is best for you, please ensure that you achieve the tension

required for the design you wish to knit.
Remember if your tension is too loose, your garment will be bigger than the pattern size and you may use more yarn. If your tension is too tight, your garment could be smaller than the pattern size and you will have yarn left over.
Furthermore if your tension is incorrect, the handle of your fabric will be too stiff or floppy and will not fit properly. It really does make sense to check your tension before starting every project.

GALLERY

BLYTH
by MARIE WALLIN
Main image page 2
Pattern page 36

BROGAN
by MARIE WALLIN
Main image page 3
Pattern page 44

FREYA
by MARIE WALLIN
Main image page 4 & 5
Pattern page 26

RHIANNON
by MARIE WALLIN
Main image page 6
Pattern page 37

PHOEBE
by MARIE WALLIN
Main image page 6 & 7
Pattern page 28

SEBASTIAN
by MARIE WALLIN
Main image page 8
Pattern page 24

JOCELYN
by MARIE WALLIN
Main image page 9
Pattern page 47

REUBEN
by MARTIN STOREY
Main image page 10
Pattern page 38

HOLLY
by MARIE WALLIN
Main image page 11
Pattern page 34

LILLITH
by MARIE WALLIN
Main image page 12 & 13
Pattern page 45

KAITLIN
by MARIE WALLIN
Main image page 14
Pattern page 30

SETH
by MARIE WALLIN
Main image page 15
Pattern page 42

LARISSA
by MARIE WALLIN
Main image page 16
Pattern page 49

FALLON
by MARIE WALLIN
Main image page 17
Pattern page 48

HERMIONE
by MARIE WALLIN
Main image page 18
Pattern page 40

RAPHAEL
by MARIE WALLIN
Main image page 19
Pattern page 51

GRACE
by MARTIN STOREY
Main image page 21
Pattern page 32

SIZE KEY

◆ SIZE 8 – 16
■ SIZE 8 – 18
● SIZE 8 – 22
▲ SIZE S – XL
◆ SIZE S – L
★ SIZE S – XXL (MENS)
✳ SIZE S-M / L / XL-XXL
✚ ACCESSORY
(Refer to pattern page)

23

SEBASTIAN

by MARIE WALLIN

Main image page 8

SIZE

	S	M	L	XL	XXL	
To fit chest						
	102	107	112	117	122	cm
	40	42	44	46	48	in

YARN

Rowan Little Big Wool

A Amber 508

| | 4 | 4 | 4 | 4 | 5 | x 50gm |

B Topaz 509

| | 4 | 5 | 5 | 5 | 6 | x 50gm |

C Jasper 505

| | 1 | 1 | 1 | 1 | 1 | x 50gm |

D Moonstone 507

| | 2 | 2 | 2 | 2 | 2 | x 50gm |

NEEDLES

1 pair 8mm (no 0) (US 11) needles
1 pair 9mm (no 00) (US 13) needles

TENSION

13 sts and 14 rows to 10 cm measured over patterned stocking stitch using 9mm (US 13) needles.

BACK

Using 8mm (US 11) needles and yarn A cast on 72 [76: 80: 84: 88] sts.
Join in yarn B.
Row 1 (RS): Using yarn A K1, *using yarn B P2, using yarn A K2, rep from * to last 3 sts, using yarn B P2, using yarn A K1.
Row 2: Using yarn A P1, *using yarn B K2, using yarn A P2, rep from * to last 3 sts, using yarn B K2, using yarn A P1.
These 2 rows form striped rib.

Work in striped rib for a further 8 rows, inc 1 st at end of last row and ending with RS facing for next row.
73 [77: 81: 85: 89] sts.
Change to 9mm (US 13) needles.
Beg and ending rows as indicated and using the **fairisle** technique as described on the information page, cont in patt from chart, which is worked entirely in st st beg with a K row, as folls:
Work straight until chart row 46 has been completed, ending with RS facing for next row. (Back should meas 39 cm.)
Shape armholes
Keeping patt correct, cast off 7 sts at beg of next 2 rows.
59 [63: 67: 71: 75] sts.
Dec 1 st at each end of next 3 [3: 1: 1: 1] rows, then on foll 2 [1: 2: 2: 1] alt rows, then on foll 4th row. 47 [53: 59: 63: 69] sts.
Cont straight until chart row 80 [82: 84: 84: 86] has been completed, ending with RS facing for next row. (Armhole should meas 24 [26: 27: 27: 29] cm.)
Shape shoulders and back neck
Next row (RS): Cast off 5 [7: 8: 9: 10] sts, patt until there are 10 [11: 12: 13: 15] sts on right needle and turn, leaving rem sts on a holder.
Work each side of neck separately.
Cast off 4 sts at beg of next row.
Cast off rem 6 [7: 8: 9: 11] sts.
With RS facing, rejoin yarns to rem sts, cast off centre 17 [17: 19: 19: 19] sts, patt to end.
Complete to match first side, reversing shapings.

FRONT

Work as given for back until 12 [12: 14: 14: 14] rows less have been worked than on back to beg of shoulder shaping, ending after chart row 68 [70: 70: 70: 72] and with RS facing for next row.
Shape neck
Next row (RS): Patt 19 [22: 25: 27: 30] sts and turn, leaving rem sts on a holder.
Work each side of neck separately.
Cast off 3 sts at beg of next row.
16 [19: 22: 24: 27] sts.
Dec 1 st at neck edge of next 3 rows, then on foll 2 [2: 3: 3: 3] alt rows.
11 [14: 16: 18: 21] sts.
Work 3 rows, ending with RS facing for next row.
Shape shoulder
Cast off 5 [7: 8: 9: 10] sts at beg of next row.
Work 1 row.
Cast off rem 6 [7: 8: 9: 11] sts.
With RS facing, rejoin yarns to rem sts, cast off centre 9 sts, patt to end.
Complete to match first side, reversing shapings.

MAKING UP

Press as described on the information page.
Join right shoulder seam using back stitch, or mattress stitch if preferred.
Neck band
With RS facing, using 8mm (US 11) needles and yarn B, pick up and knit 14 [14: 15: 15: 15] sts down left side of neck, 9 sts from front, 14 [14: 15: 15: 15] sts up right side of neck, then 25 [25: 27: 27: 27] sts from back.

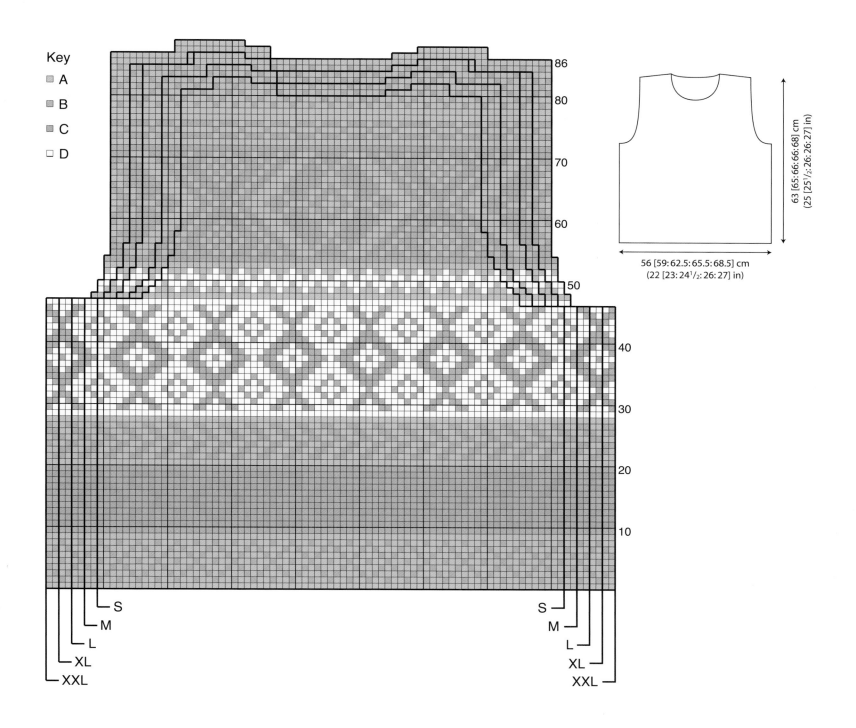

Key
- ■ A
- ■ B
- ■ C
- □ D

63 [65: 66: 66: 68] cm
(25 [25¹/₂: 26: 26: 27] in)

56 [59: 62.5: 65.5: 68.5] cm
(22 [23: 24¹/₂: 26: 27] in)

62 [62: 66: 66: 66] sts.
Join in yarn A.
Row 1 (WS): Using yarn B K2, ★using yarn A P2, using yarn B K2, rep from ★ to end.
Row 2: Using yarn B P2, ★using yarn A K2, using yarn B P2, rep from ★ to end.
These 2 rows form striped rib.

Work in striped rib for a further 2 rows, ending with **WS** facing for next row.
Cast off in rib.
Join left shoulder and neck band seam.
Armhole borders (both alike)
With RS facing, using 8mm (US 11) needles and yarn B, pick up and knit 70 [74: 78: 78: 82]

sts evenly all round armhole edge.
Join in yarn A and work in striped rib as given for neck band for 4 rows, ending with **WS** facing for next row.
Cast off in rib.
See information page for finishing instructions.

FREYA

by MARIE WALLIN

Main image page 4 & 5

SIZE

8	10	12	14	16	18	
To fit bust						
82	87	92	97	102	107	cm
32	34	36	38	40	42	in

YARN

Rowan Biggy Print

A Shadow 265

8	8	9	10	10	11	x 100gm

B Leafy Lane 263

3	3	3	3	4	4	x 100gm

C Biscuit 266

3	3	4	4	4	4	x 100gm

D Jewel 264

3	3	3	3	3	3	x 100gm

NEEDLES

1 pair 10mm (no 000) (US 15) needles
1 pair 12mm (US 17) needles

BUTTONS – 8 x 00411

TENSION

7 sts and 10 rows to 10 cm measured over stocking stitch using 12mm (US 17) needles.

BACK

Using 12mm (US 17) needles and yarn A cast on 34 [36: 38: 40: 42: 44] sts.

Row 1 (RS): K0 [0: 0: 1: 0: 0], P0 [1: 2: 2: 0: 1], ★K2, P2, rep from ★ to last 2 [3: 0: 1: 2: 3] sts, K2 [2: 0: 1: 2: 2], P0 [1: 0: 0: 0: 1].
Row 2: P0 [0: 0: 1: 0: 0], K0 [1: 2: 2: 0: 1], ★P2, K2, rep from ★ to last 2 [3: 0: 1: 2: 3] sts, P2 [2: 0: 1: 2: 2], K0 [1: 0: 0: 0: 1].
These 2 rows form rib.

Work in rib for a further 6 rows, ending with RS facing for next row.
Joining in colours as required and beg with a K row, work in striped st st as folls:
Rows 1 and 2: Using yarn A.
Rows 3 and 4: Using yarn B, dec 1 st at each end of first of these rows.
32 [34: 36: 38: 40: 42] sts.
Rows 5 to 8: Using yarn C, dec 1 st at each end of 3rd of these rows.
30 [32: 34: 36: 38: 40] sts.
Rows 9 and 10: Using yarn A.
Rows 11 and 12: Using yarn D.
Rows 13 and 14: Using yarn A, inc 1 st at each end of first of these rows.
32 [34: 36: 38: 40: 42] sts.
Rows 15 to 17: Using yarn B.
Rows 18 and 19: Using yarn D.
Row 20: Using yarn C.
These 20 rows form striped st st and shape side seams.
Cont in striped st st, inc 1 st at each end of next row.
34 [36: 38: 40: 42: 44] sts.
Cont straight until back meas 34 [34: 33: 36: 35: 37] cm, ending with RS facing for next row.

Shape armholes

Keeping stripes correct, cast off 3 sts at beg of next 2 rows.
28 [30: 32: 34: 36: 38] sts.
Dec 1 st at each end of next and foll 0 [1: 1: 2: 2: 3] alt rows.
26 [26: 28: 28: 30: 30] sts.
Cont straight until armhole meas 22 [22: 23: 23: 24: 24] cm, ending with RS facing for next row.

Shape shoulders and back neck

Next row (RS): Cast off 3 sts, K until there are 6 [6: 7: 7: 7: 7] sts on right needle and turn, leaving rem sts on a holder.
Work each side of neck separately.
Cast off 3 sts at beg of next row.
Cast off rem 3 [3: 4: 4: 4: 4] sts.
With RS facing, rejoin appropriate yarn to rem sts, cast off centre 8 [8: 8: 8: 10: 10] sts, K to end.
Complete to match first side, reversing shapings.

LEFT FRONT

Using 12mm (US 17) needles and yarn A cast on 14 [15: 16: 17: 18: 19] sts.

Row 1 (RS): K0 [0: 0: 1: 0: 0], P0 [1: 2: 2: 0: 1], ★K2, P2, rep from ★ to last 2 sts, K2.
Row 2: ★P2, K2, rep from ★ to last 2 [3: 0: 1: 2: 3] sts, P2 [2: 0: 1: 2: 2], K0 [1: 0: 0: 0: 1].
These 2 rows form rib.
Work in rib for a further 6 rows, ending with RS facing for next row.
Joining in colours as required and beg with a K row, work in striped st st as given for back, dec 1 st at beg of 3rd and foll 4th row.
12 [13: 14: 15: 16: 17] sts.
Work 5 rows.
Inc 1 st at beg of next and foll 8th row.
14 [15: 16: 17: 18: 19] sts.
Cont straight until left front matches back to beg of armhole shaping, ending with RS facing for next row.

Shape armhole

Keeping stripes correct, cast off 3 sts at beg

of next row.

11 [12: 13: 14: 15: 16] sts.

Work 1 row.

Dec 1 st at armhole edge of next and foll 0 [1: 1: 2: 2: 3] alt rows.

10 [10: 11: 11: 12: 12] sts.

Cont straight until 7 rows less have been worked than on back to beg of shoulders shaping, ending with **WS** facing for next row.

Shape neck

Keeping stripes correct, cast off 2 [2: 2: 2: 3: 3] sts at beg of next row.

8 [8: 9: 9: 9: 9] sts.

Dec 1 st at neck edge of next and foll alt row.

6 [6: 7: 7: 7: 7] sts.

Work 3 rows, ending with RS facing for next row.

Shape shoulder

Cast off 3 sts at beg of next row.

Work 1 row.

Cast off rem 3 [3: 4: 4: 4: 4] sts.

RIGHT FRONT

Using 12mm (US 17) needles and yarn A cast on 14 [15: 16: 17: 18: 19] sts.

Row 1 (RS): ★K2, P2, rep from ★ to last 2 [3: 0: 1: 2: 3] sts, K2 [2: 0: 1: 2: 2], P0 [1: 0: 0: 0: 1].

Row 2: P0 [0: 0: 1: 0: 0], K0 [1: 2: 2: 0: 1], ★P2, K2, rep from ★ to last 2 sts, P2.

These 2 rows form rib.

Work in rib for a further 6 rows, ending with RS facing for next row.

Joining in colours as required and beg with a K row, work in striped st st as given for back, dec 1 st at end of 3rd and foll 4th row.

12 [13: 14: 15: 16: 17] sts.

Complete to match left front, reversing shapings.

SLEEVES

Using 12mm (US 17) needles and yarn A cast on 20 [20: 22: 22: 24: 24] sts.

Row 1 (RS): K0 [0: 0: 0: 1: 1], P1 [1: 2: 2: 2: 2], ★K2, P2, rep from ★ to last 3 [3: 0: 0: 1: 1] sts, K2 [2: 0: 0: 1: 1], P1 [1: 0: 0: 0: 0].

Row 2: P0 [0: 0: 0: 1: 1], K1 [1: 2: 2: 2: 2], ★P2, K2, rep from ★ to last 3 [3: 0: 0: 1: 1] sts, P2 [2: 0: 0: 1: 1], K1 [1: 0: 0: 0: 0].

These 2 rows form rib.

Work in rib for a further 6 rows, ending with RS facing for next row.

Joining in colours as required and beg with a K row, work in striped st st as given for back, shaping sides by inc 1 st at each end of next and every foll 10th row to 28 [28: 30: 30: 32: 32] sts.

Cont straight until sleeve meas 44 [44: 45: 45: 46: 46] cm, ending with RS facing for next row.

Shape top

Keeping stripes correct, cast off 3 sts at beg of next 2 rows.

22 [22: 24: 24: 26: 26] sts.

Dec 1 st at each end of next and every foll 4th row to 16 [16: 18: 18: 20: 20] sts, then on every foll alt row to 12 sts, then on foll row, ending with RS facing for next row.

Cast off rem 10 sts.

MAKING UP

Press as described on the information page.

Join both shoulder seams using back stitch, or mattress stitch if preferred.

Button band

With RS facing, using 10mm (US 15) needles and yarn A, beg at neck edge, pick up and knit 38 [38: 38: 42: 42: 46] sts down left front opening edge to cast-on edge.

Row 1 (WS): P2, ★K2, P2, rep from ★ to end.

Row 2: K2, ★P2, K2, rep from ★ to end.

These 2 rows form rib.

Work in rib for a further 9 rows, ending with RS facing for next row.

Cast off in rib.

Buttonhole band

Work as given for button band, picking up sts up right front opening edge and with the addition of 2 sets of 4 buttonholes in rows 2 and 8 as folls:

Buttonhole row (RS): Rib 4 [4: 4: 3: 3: 3], ★yrn (to make a buttonhole), work 2 tog, rib 8 [8: 8: 10: 10: 11], rep from ★ twice more, yrn (to make 4th buttonhole), work 2 tog, rib 2 [2: 2: 1: 1: 2].

Collar

With RS facing, using 10mm (US 15) needles and yarn A, beg and ending at front band pick-up rows, pick up and knit 12 [12: 12: 12: 13: 13] sts up right side of neck, 14 [14: 14: 14: 16: 16] sts from back, then 12 [12: 12: 12: 13: 13] sts down left side of neck.

38 [38: 38: 38: 42: 42] sts.

Work in rib as given for button band for 13 cm.

Cast off in rib.

See information page for finishing instructions, setting in sleeves using the set-in method.

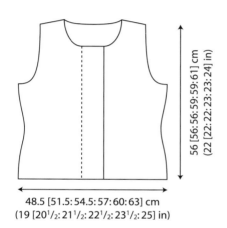

48.5 [51.5: 54.5: 57: 60: 63] cm
(19 [20½: 21½: 22½: 23½: 25] in)

56 [56: 56: 59: 59: 61] cm
(22 [22: 22: 23: 23: 24] in)

44 [44: 45: 45: 46: 46] cm
(17½ [17½: 17½: 17½: 18: 18] in)

PHOEBE

by MARIE WALLIN

Main image page 6 & 7

SIZE

	S	M	L	XL	
To fit bust					
	82-87	92-97	102-107	112-117	cm
	32-34	36-38	40-42	44-46	in

YARN

Rowan Little Big Wool

	13	14	14	15	x 50gm

(photographed in Jasper 505)

CROCHET HOOK

8.00mm (no 0) (US L11) crochet hook

TENSION

10 sts and 7 rows to 10 cm measured over pattern using 8.00mm (US L11) hook.

UK CROCHET ABBREVIATIONS

ch = chain; **dc** = double crochet; **sp(s)** = space(es); **ss** = slip stitch; **tr(s)** = treble(s); **dc2tog** = *insert hook as indicated, yoh and draw loop through, rep from * once more, yoh and draw through all 3 loops on hook; **tr2tog** = *yoh and insert hook as indicated, yoh and draw loop through, yoh and draw through 2 loops, rep from * once more, yoh and draw through all 3 loops on hook; **yoh** = yarn over hook.

US CROCHET ABBREVIATIONS

ch = chain; **dc** = single crochet; **sp(s)** = space(es); **ss** = slip stitch; **tr(s)** = double(s); **dc2tog** = *insert hook as indicated, yoh and draw loop through, rep from * once more, yoh and draw through all 3 loops on hook; **tr2tog** = *yoh and insert hook as indicated, yoh and draw loop through, yoh and draw through 2 loops, rep from * once more, yoh and draw through all 3 loops on hook; **yoh** = yarn over hook.

BACK

Using 8.00mm (US L11) hook make 54 [59: 64: 69] ch.

Foundation row (RS): 1 tr into 4th ch from hook, *3 ch, miss 3 ch, 1 tr into each of next 2 ch, rep from * to end, turn.
52 [57: 62: 67] sts.
Cont in patt as folls:

Row 1 (WS): 3 ch (counts as first tr), miss tr at base of 3 ch and next tr, *5 tr into next ch sp**, miss 2 tr, rep from * to end, ending last rep at **, miss 1 tr, 1 tr into top of 3 ch at beg of previous row, turn.

Row 2: 3 ch (counts as first tr), miss tr at base of 3 ch, 1 tr into next tr, *3 ch, miss 3 tr, 1 tr into each of next 2 tr, rep from * to end, working last tr into top of 3 ch at beg of previous row, turn.

Rows 3 and 4: As rows 1 and 2.

Row 5: As row 1.

Row 6: 1 ch (does NOT count as st), 1 dc into each tr to end, working last dc into top of 3 ch at beg of previous row, turn.

Row 7: 1 ch (does NOT count as st), 1 dc into each dc to end, turn.

Row 8: As row 7.

Row 9: 4 ch (counts as first tr and 1 ch), miss dc at base of 4 ch and next dc, 1 tr into next dc, *1 ch, miss 1 dc, 1 tr into next dc, rep from * to last 3 [2: 3: 2] dc, 1 ch, miss 1 dc, 1 tr into each of last 2 [1: 2: 1] dc, turn.

Row 10: 3 ch (counts as first tr), miss tr at base of 3 ch, (1 tr into next tr) 1 [0: 1: 0] times, *1 ch, miss 1 ch, 1 tr into next tr, rep from * to end, working tr at end of last rep into 3rd of 4 ch at beg of previous row, turn.

Row 11: 1 ch (does NOT count as st), 1 dc into each tr and ch sp to end, working last dc into top of 3 ch at beg of previous row, turn.

Rows 12 and 13: As row 7.

Row 14: 3 ch (counts as first tr), miss dc at base of 3 ch, 1 tr into next dc, *3 ch, miss 3 dc, 1 tr into each of next 2 dc, rep from * to end, turn.

These 14 rows form patt.

Work in patt for a further 14 rows, ending after patt row 14 and with **WS** facing for next row. (Back should meas 41 cm.)

Shape armholes

Row 1 (WS): ss across and into centre of first ch sp, 3 ch (counts as first tr), 1 tr into same ch sp, *miss 2 tr, 5 tr into next ch sp, rep from * to 7 sts, miss 2 tr, 2 tr into last ch sp and turn, leaving rem sts unworked.
44 [49: 54: 59] sts.

Row 2: 3 ch (does NOT count as st), miss tr at base of 3 ch, 1 tr into next tr, *1 tr into next tr, 3 ch, miss 3 tr, 1 tr into next tr, rep from * to last 2 sts, tr2tog over last 2 sts, turn.
42 [47: 52: 57] sts.

Row 3: 3 ch (does NOT count as st), miss tr2tog at base of 3 ch and next tr, *5 tr into next ch sp, miss 2 tr, rep from * to last ch sp, 4 tr into last ch sp, tr2tog working first "leg" into last ch sp and second "leg" into tr at beg of previous row, turn.

40 [45: 50: 55] sts.

Row 4: 3 ch (does NOT count as st), miss tr2tog at base of 3 ch, 1 tr into next tr, 2 ch, miss 2 tr, ★1 tr into each of next 2 tr, 3 ch, miss 3 tr, rep from ★ to last 6 sts, 1 tr into each of next 2 tr, 2 ch, miss 2 tr, tr2tog over next 2 tr, turn. 38 [43: 48: 53] sts.

Row 5: 3 ch (does NOT count as st), miss tr2tog at base of 3 ch, 3 tr into first ch sp, ★miss 2 tr, 5 tr into next ch sp, rep from ★ until 1 ch sp remains at end of row, miss 2 tr, 2 tr into last ch sp, tr2tog working first "leg" into last ch sp and second "leg" into tr at beg of previous row, turn.

36 [41: 46: 51] sts.

Row 6: 1 ch (does NOT count as st), dc2tog over tr2tog at end of previous row and next tr, 1 dc into each tr to last 2 sts, dc2tog over last 2 tr, turn. 34 [39: 44: 49] sts.

Last 5 rows set decreases. At beg of rows, work turning ch as normal but this does NOT count as st, thereby dec 1 st, and should NOT be worked into on foll row. At end of rows, replace last 2 sts with either a dc2tog or a tr2tog (depending on patt row), thereby dec 1 st.

Working all shaping as now set, dec 1 st at each end of next 0 [1: 2: 3] rows. 34 [37: 40: 43] sts. Cont straight until armhole meas 23 [24: 25: 26] cm.
Fasten off.

LEFT FRONT

Using 8.00mm (US L11) hook make 29 [29: 35: 35] ch.
Work foundation row as given for back.
27 [27: 33: 33] sts.
Work in patt as given for M size of back for 25 rows, ending after patt row 11 and with RS facing for next row.

Shape front slope

Next row (RS): 1 ch (does NOT count as st), 1 dc into each dc to last 2 dc, dc2tog over last 2 dc, turn.
26 [26: 32: 32] sts.
Now working all shaping as set by back armholes, dec 1 st at front slope edge of next [2nd: next: 2nd] and foll 1 [0: 1: 0] rows, ending with **WS** facing for next row.
24 [25: 30: 31] sts.

Shape armhole

Dec 1 [0: 1: 0] st at beg (front slope edge) and dec 4 sts at end (armhole edge) of next row.
19 [21: 25: 27] sts.
Dec 1 st at armhole edge of next 5 [6: 7: 8] rows **and at same time** dec 1 st at front slope edge of 2nd [next: next: next] and foll 0 [0: 1: 0] rows, then on foll 5 [3: 6: 7] alt rows, then

on 0 [2: 0: 0] foll 3rd rows. 8 [9: 10: 11] sts.
Cont straight until left front matches back to fasten-off point.
Fasten off.

RIGHT FRONT

Work to match left front, reversing all shapings.

SLEEVES

Using 8.00mm (US L11) hook make 27 [27: 32: 32] ch.

Row 1 (RS): 1 tr into 8th ch from hook, 1 tr into next ch, ★3 ch, miss 3 ch, 1 tr into each of next 2 ch, rep from ★ to last 3 ch, 2 ch, miss 2 ch, 1 tr into last ch, turn.
23 [23: 28: 28] sts.

Row 2: 3 ch (counts as first tr), miss tr at base of 3 ch, 3 tr into first ch sp, (miss 2 tr, 5 tr into next ch sp) 3 [3: 4: 4] times, miss 2 tr, 4 tr into last ch sp, turn.

Row 3: 3 ch (counts as first tr), 1 tr into tr at base of 3 ch, 2 ch, miss 2 tr, (1 tr into each of next 2 tr, 3 ch, miss 3 tr) 3 [3: 4: 4] times, 1 tr into each of next 2 tr, 2 ch, miss 2 tr, 2 tr into top of 3 ch at beg of previous row, turn.
25 [25: 30: 30] sts.

Row 4: 3 ch (counts as first tr), miss tr at base of 3 ch, 1 tr into next tr, 3 tr into first ch sp, (miss 2 tr, 5 tr into next ch sp) 3 [3: 4: 4] times, miss 2 tr, 3 tr into last ch sp, 1 tr into next tr, 1 tr into top of 3 ch at beg of previous row, turn.

Row 5: 3 ch (counts as first tr), 1 tr into tr at base of 3 ch, (3 ch, miss 3 tr, 1 tr into each of next 2 tr) 4 [4: 5: 5] times, 3 ch, miss 3 tr, 2 tr into top of 3 ch at beg of previous row, turn.
27 [27: 32: 32] sts.

Row 6: 3 ch (counts as first tr), miss tr at base of 3 ch and next tr, 5 tr into first ch sp, (miss 2 tr, 5 tr into next ch sp) 4 [4: 5: 5] times, miss 1 tr, 1 tr into top of 3 ch at beg of previous row, turn.

Row 7: 1 ch (does NOT count as st), 2 dc into first tr, 1 dc into each tr to last st, 2 dc into top of 3 ch at beg of previous row, turn.
29 [29: 34: 34] sts.

Row 8: 1 ch (does NOT count as st), 1 dc into each dc to end, turn.

Row 9: 1 ch (does NOT count as st), 2 dc into first dc, 1 dc into each dc to last dc, 2 dc into last dc, turn.
31 [31: 36: 36] sts.

Row 10: 3 ch (counts as first tr), miss dc at base of 3 ch, 1 tr into next dc, ★1 ch, miss 1 dc, 1 tr into next dc, rep from ★ to last dc, 1 tr into last dc, turn.

Row 11: 4 ch (counts as first tr and 1 ch), miss tr at base of 4 ch, 1 tr into next tr, ★1 ch, miss 1 ch, 1 tr into next tr, rep from ★ to last st, 1

ch, 1 tr into top of 3 ch at beg of previous row, turn.
33 [33: 38: 38] sts.

Row 12: 1 ch (does NOT count as st), 1 dc into each tr and ch sp to end, working last dc into 3rd of 4 ch at beg of previous row, turn.

Row 13: As row 9. 35 [35: 40: 40] sts.

Row 14: As row 8.

Row 15: 3 ch (counts as first tr), 1 tr into dc at base of 3 ch, ★3 ch, miss 3 dc, 1 tr into each of next 2 dc, rep from ★ to last 4 dc, 3 ch, miss 3 dc, 2 tr into last dc, turn.
37 [37: 42: 42] sts.

Rows 2 to 15 form patt and beg sleeve shaping.
Working all increases as now set, inc 1 st at each end of 2nd and every foll alt row until there are 45 [47: 50: 52] sts, taking inc sts into patt.
Cont straight until sleeve meas 43 [44: 45: 45] cm.

Shape top

Working all shaping as set by back armholes, dec 4 sts at each end of next row.
37 [39: 42: 44] sts.
Dec 1 st at each end of next 7 [8: 9: 10] rows.
23 [23: 24: 24] sts.
Fasten off.

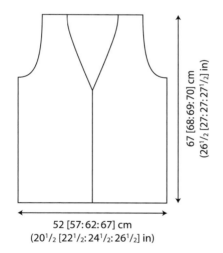

67 [68: 69: 70] cm
(26¹/₂ [27: 27: 27¹/₂] in)

52 [57: 62: 67] cm
(20¹/₂ [22¹/₂: 24¹/₂: 26¹/₂] in)

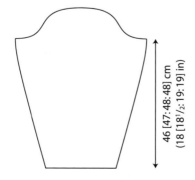

46 [47: 48: 48] cm
(18 [18¹/₂: 19: 19] in)

MAKING UP

Press as described on the information page.
Join shoulder seams. Join side seams.

Front border

With RS facing and using 8.00mm (US L11) hook, attach yarn at base of right front opening edge, 1 ch (does NOT count as st), work in dc evenly up entire right front opening and neck edge, across back neck and down left front slope and opening edge to base of left front opening edge, turn.

Row 1 (WS): 1 ch (does NOT count as st), 1 dc into each dc to end, turn.

This row forms dc fabric.

Work in dc fabric for a further 2 rows, but do NOT turn at end of last row, so ending with WS facing for next row.

Do NOT fasten off.

Hem edging

With **WS** facing and using 8.00mm (US L11) hook, 1 ch (does NOT count as st), now work in dc evenly across entire lower edge of fronts and back, ending at lower edge of right front opening edge and ensuring there is a multiple of 4 dc plus 1, turn.

Next row (RS): 1 ch (does NOT count as st), 1 dc into first dc, *miss 1 dc, 5 tr into next dc, miss 1 dc, 1 dc into next dc, rep from * to end. Fasten off.

Cuff edgings (both alike)

With **WS** facing and using 8.00mm (US L11) hook, 1 ch (does NOT count as st), now work in dc evenly across entire lower edge of sleeve, ensuring there is a multiple of 4 dc plus 1, turn.

Next row (RS): 1 ch (does NOT count as st), 1 dc into first dc, *miss 1 dc, 5 tr into next dc, miss 1 dc, 1 dc into next dc, rep from * to end. Fasten off.

Belt

Using 8.00mm (US L11) hook make a ch approx 135 cm long.

Row 1 (RS): 1 dc into 2nd ch from hook, 1 dc into each ch to end, turn.

Work in dc fabric as given for front border for 3 rows.

Fasten off.

See information page for finishing instructions, setting in sleeves using the set-in method.

KAITLIN

by MARIE WALLIN

Main image page 14

SIZE

	S	M	L	
To fit bust				
	82–87	92–97	102–107	cm
	32–34	36–38	40–42	in

YARN

Rowan Little Big Wool

	15	17	18	x 50gm

(photographed in Pearl 500)

NEEDLES

1 pair 9mm (no 00) (US 13) needles

8.00mm (no 0) (US L11) crochet hook

TENSION

12½ sts and 16 rows to 10 cm measured over pattern using 9mm (US 13) needles.

UK CROCHET ABBREVIATIONS

ch = chain; **dc** = double crochet;
sp = space; **tr** = treble.

US CROCHET ABBREVIATIONS

ch = chain; **dc** = single crochet;
sp = space; **tr** = double

BACK

Using 9mm (US 13) needles cast on 85 [91: 97] sts.

Row 1 (RS): (K1, K2tog, yfwd) 0 [1: 0] times, K1, *yfwd, sl 1, K1, psso, K1, K2tog, yfwd, K1, rep from * to last 0 [3: 0] sts, (yfwd, sl 1, K1, psso, K1) 0 [1: 0] times.

Row 2 and every foll alt row: Purl.

Row 3: (K2tog, K1, yfwd) 0 [1: 0] times, K1, *yfwd, K1, sl 1, K2tog, psso, K1, yfwd, K1, rep from * to last 0 [3: 0] sts, (yfwd, K1, sl 1, K1, psso) 0 [1: 0] times.

Row 5: (K1, yfwd, sl 1, K1, psso) 0 [1: 0] times, K1, ★K2tog, yfwd, K1, yfwd, sl 1, K1, psso, K1, rep from ★ to last 0 [3: 0] sts, (K2tog, yfwd, K1) 0 [1: 0] times.

Row 7: (K2tog, K1, yfwd) 1 [0: 1] times, K1, ★yfwd, K1, sl 1, K2tog, psso, K1, yfwd, K1, rep from ★ to last 3 [0: 3] sts, (yfwd, K1, sl 1, K1, psso) 1 [0: 1] times.

Row 8: As row 2.

These 8 rows form patt.

Cont in patt until back meas 33 [34: 35] cm, ending with RS facing for next row.

Shape armhole openings

Inc 1 st at each end of next and foll 2 alt rows, then on foll 3 rows, taking inc sts into patt and ending with RS facing for next row.
97 [103: 109] sts.

Place markers at both ends of last row to denote base of armholes.

Cont straight until armhole meas 21 [22: 23] cm **from markers**, ending with RS facing for next row.

Shape shoulders and back neck

Cast off 12 [13: 13] sts at beg of next 2 rows.
73 [77: 83] sts.

Next row (RS): Cast off 12 [13: 13] sts, patt until there are 15 [16: 18] sts on right needle and turn, leaving rem sts on a holder.

Work each side of neck separately.

Cast off 4 sts at beg of next row.

Cast off rem 11 [12: 14] sts.

With RS facing, rejoin yarn to rem sts, cast off centre 19 [19: 21] sts, patt to end.

Complete to match first side, reversing shapings.

LEFT FRONT

Using 9mm (US 13) needles cast on 37 [40: 43] sts.

Row 1 (RS): (K1, K2tog, yfwd) 0 [1: 0] times, K1, ★yfwd, sl 1, K1, psso, K1, K2tog, yfwd, K1, rep from ★ to end.

Row 2 and every foll alt row: Purl.

Row 3: (K2tog, K1, yfwd) 0 [1: 0] times, K1, ★yfwd, K1, sl 1, K2tog, psso, K1, yfwd, K1, rep from ★ to end.

Row 5: (K1, yfwd, sl 1, K1, psso) 0 [1: 0] times, K1, ★K2tog, yfwd, K1, yfwd, sl 1, K1, psso, K1, rep from ★ to end.

Row 7: (K2tog, K1, yfwd) 1 [0: 1] times, K1, ★yfwd, K1, sl 1, K2tog, psso, K1, yfwd, K1, rep from ★ to last 3 sts, yfwd, K1, sl 1, K1, psso.

Row 8: As row 2.

These 8 rows form patt.

Cont in patt until left front matches back to beg of armhole opening shaping, ending with RS facing for next row.

Shape armhole opening

Inc 1 st at beg of next and foll alt row.
39 [42: 45] sts.

Work 1 row, ending with RS facing for next row.

Shape front slope

Keeping patt correct, inc 1 st at beg of next row and at same edge on foll 3 rows **and at same time** dec 1 st at end of next row, ending with RS facing for next row.
42 [45: 48] sts.

Place markers at end of last row to denote base of armhole.

Dec 1 st at front slope edge **only** of next and 4 [3: 6] foll 4th rows, then on 2 [3: 1] foll 6th rows. 35 [38: 40] sts.

Cont straight until left front matches back to beg of shoulder shaping, ending with RS facing for next row.

Shape shoulder

Cast off 12 [13: 13] sts at beg of next and foll alt row.

Work 1 row.

Cast off rem 11 [12: 14] sts.

RIGHT FRONT

Using 9mm (US 13) needles cast on 37 [40: 43] sts.

Row 1 (RS): K1, ★yfwd, sl 1, K1, psso, K1, K2tog, yfwd, K1, rep from ★ to last 0 [3: 0] sts, (yfwd, sl 1, K1, psso, K1) 0 [1: 0] times.

Row 2 and every foll alt row: Purl.

Row 3: K1, ★yfwd, K1, sl 1, K2tog, psso, K1, yfwd, K1, rep from ★ to last 0 [3: 0] sts, (yfwd, K1, sl 1, K1, psso) 0 [1: 0] times.

Row 5: K1, ★K2tog, yfwd, K1, yfwd, sl 1, K1, psso, K1, rep from ★ to last 0 [3: 0] sts, (K2tog, yfwd, K1) 0 [1: 0] times.

Row 7: K2tog, K1, yfwd, K1, ★yfwd, K1, sl 1, K2tog, psso, K1, yfwd, K1, rep from ★ to last 3 [0: 3] sts, (yfwd, K1, sl 1, K1, psso) 1 [0: 1] times.

Row 8: As row 2.

These 8 rows form patt.

Complete to match left front, reversing shapings.

MAKING UP

Press as described on the information page.

Join both shoulder seams using back stitch, or mattress stitch if preferred.

Front band

With RS facing and using 8.00mm (US L11) crochet hook, attach yarn at base of right front opening edge and, working evenly up entire right front opening edge, across back neck, then down entire left front opening edge to cast-on edge, cont as folls:

Row 1 (RS): 1 ch (does NOT count as st), 2 dc into edge, ★3 ch, miss approx 2.5 cm along edge, work 3 dc into edge, rep from ★ to end, ending last rep with 2 dc instead of 3 dc (and ensuring last dc is worked into left front opening edge corner point), turn.

Row 2: 1 ch (does NOT count as st), 1 dc into first dc, ★miss 1 dc, 5 tr into next ch sp, miss 1 dc, 1 dc into next dc, rep from ★ to end, turn.

Row 3: 4 ch (counts as 1 tr and 1 ch), miss dc at end of last row and next tr, ★1 dc into each of next 3 tr★★, 3 ch, miss (1 tr, 1 dc and 1 tr), rep from ★ to end, ending last rep at ★★, 1 ch, miss 1 tr, 1 tr into dc at beg of previous row, turn.

Row 4: 3 ch (counts as first tr), miss tr at end of previous row, 2 tr into first ch sp, ★miss 1 dc, 1 dc into next dc, miss 1 dc★★, 5 tr into next ch sp, rep from ★ to end, ending last rep at ★★, 2 tr into last ch sp, 1 tr into 3rd of 4 ch at beg of previous row, turn.

Row 5: 1 ch (does NOT count as st), 1 dc into each of first 2 tr, ★3 ch, miss (1 tr, 1 dc and 1 tr)★★, 1 dc into each of next 3 tr, rep from ★ to end, ending last rep at ★★, 1 dc into next tr, 1 dc into top of 3 ch at beg of previous row, turn.

Rows 6 to 9: As rows 2 to 5.

Row 10: As row 2.

Fasten off.

See information page for finishing instructions.

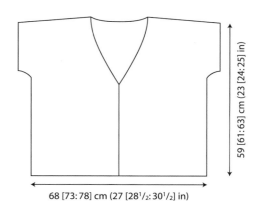

68 [73: 78] cm (27 [28½: 30½] in)

59 [61:63] cm (23 [24:25] in)

31

GRACE

by MARTIN STOREY

Main image page 21

SIZE

8	10	12	14	16	18	20	22	

To fit bust

82	87	92	97	102	107	112	117	cm
32	34	36	38	40	42	44	46	in

YARN

Rowan Little Big Wool

14	14	15	15	16	16	17	17	x 50gm

(photographed in Quartz 506)

NEEDLES

1 pair 8mm (no 0) (US 11) needles
1 pair 9mm (no 00) (US 13) needles
Cable needle

TENSION

11 sts and 15 rows to 10 cm measured over stocking stitch using 9mm (US 13) needles.

SPECIAL ABBREVIATIONS

C4B = slip next 2 sts onto cable needle and leave at back of work, K2, then K2 from cable needle; **C4F** = slip next 2 sts onto cable needle and leave at front of work, K2, then K2 from cable needle; **loop 6 tog** = with yarn at back (WS) of work insert right needle between 6th and 7th sts on left needle and draw loop through, place this loop on left needle and K tog this loop with first st on left needle, K1, P2, K2.

BACK

Using 8mm (US 11) needles cast on 80 [82: 86: 88: 92: 94: 98: 102] sts.
Row 1 (RS): P1 [2: 0: 1: 3: 0: 2: 0], *K2, P2, rep from * to last 3 [0: 2: 3: 1: 2: 0: 0] sts, K2 [0: 2: 2: 0: 2: 0: 0], P1 [0: 0: 1: 1: 0: 0: 0].
Row 2: K1 [2: 0: 1: 3: 0: 2: 0], *P2, K2, rep from * to last 3 [0: 2: 3: 1: 2: 0: 0] sts, P2 [0: 2: 2: 0: 2: 0: 0], K1 [0: 0: 1: 1: 0: 0: 0].
These 2 rows form rib.
Keeping rib correct, cont as folls:
Row 3: Rib 1 [2: 4: 5: 7: 8: 2: 4], *loop 6 tog, rib 2, rep from * to last 7 [0: 2: 3: 5: 6: 0: 2] sts, (loop 6 tog) 1 [0: 0: 0: 0: 0: 0: 0] times, rib 1 [0: 2: 3: 5: 6: 0: 2].
Work 3 rows.
Row 7: Rib 5 [6: 8: 1: 3: 4: 6: 8], *loop 6 tog, rib 2, rep from * to last 3 [4: 6: 7: 1: 2: 4: 6] sts, (loop 6 tog) 0 [0: 0: 1: 0: 0: 0: 0] times, rib 3 [4: 6: 1: 1: 2: 4: 6].
Work 1 row.
Last 8 rows form smocked rib.
Cont in smocked rib for a further 5 rows, ending with **WS** facing for next row.
Row 14 (WS): Rib 0 [1: 2: 3: 0: 1: 3: 0], (work 2 tog, rib 3 [3: 3: 3: 4: 4: 4: 5]) 5 times, rib 30, (rib 3 [3: 3: 3: 4: 4: 4: 5], work 2 tog) 5 times, rib 0 [1: 2: 3: 0: 1: 3: 0].
70 [72: 76: 78: 82: 84: 88: 92] sts.
Change to 9mm (US 13) needles.
Keeping centre 30 sts correct in smocked rib as set, now work cable patt over edge sts as folls:
Row 1 (RS): P4 [5: 6: 7: 9: 10: 12: 14], (K4, P4) twice, rib 30, (P4, K4) twice, P to end.
Row 2: K4 [5: 6: 7: 9: 10: 12: 14], (P4, K4) twice, rib 30, (K4, P4) twice, K to end.
Row 3: P4 [5: 6: 7: 9: 10: 12: 14], (C4B, P4) twice, rib 30, (P4, C4F) twice, P to end.
Row 4: As row 2.
These 4 rows form patt.
Cont in patt until back meas 39 [38: 38: 39:

39: 40: 40: 41] cm, ending with RS facing for next row.
Shape raglan armholes
Keeping patt correct, cast off 3 sts at beg of next 2 rows.
64 [66: 70: 72: 76: 78: 82: 86] sts.
Dec 1 st at each end of next 1 [1: 1: 1: 3: 3: 7: 9] rows, then on 2 [2: 0: 0: 0: 0: 0: 0] foll 4th rows, then on every foll alt row until 34 [34: 34: 34: 36: 36: 36: 36] sts rem.
Work 1 row, ending with RS facing for next row.
Break yarn and leave sts on a holder.

FRONT

Work as given for back until 44 [44: 44: 44: 46: 46: 46: 46] sts rem in raglan armhole shaping.
Work 1 row, ending with RS facing for next row.
Shape neck
Next row (RS): Work 2 tog, patt 8 sts and turn, leaving rem sts on a holder.
Work each side of neck separately.
Keeping patt correct, dec 1 st at neck edge of next 5 rows **and at same time** dec 1 st at raglan armhole edge of 2nd and foll alt row.
2 sts.
Next row (RS): Work 2 tog and fasten off.
With RS facing, slip centre 24 [24: 24: 24: 26: 26: 26: 26] sts onto a holder, rejoin yarn to rem sts, patt to last 2 sts, work 2 tog.
Complete to match first side, reversing shapings.

SLEEVES

Using 8mm (US 11) needles cast on 50 [50:

52: 52: 54: 54: 56: 56] sts.

Row 1 (RS): P2 [2: 3: 3: 0: 0: 1: 1], ★K2, P2, rep from ★ to last 0 [0: 1: 1: 2: 2: 3: 3] sts, K0 [0: 1: 1: 2: 2: 2: 2], P0 [0: 0: 0: 0: 0: 1: 1].

Row 2: K2 [2: 3: 3: 0: 0: 1: 1], ★P2, K2, rep from ★ to last 0 [0: 1: 1: 2: 2: 3: 3] sts, P0 [0: 1: 1: 2: 2: 2: 2], K0 [0: 0: 0: 0: 0: 1: 1].

These 2 rows form rib.

Keeping rib correct, cont as folls:

Row 3: Rib 2 [2: 3: 3: 4: 4: 5: 5], ★loop 6 tog, rib 2, rep from ★ to last 0 [0: 1: 1: 2: 2: 3: 3] sts, rib 0 [0: 1: 1: 2: 2: 3: 3].

Work 3 rows.

Row 7: Rib 6 [6: 7: 7: 8: 8: 1: 1], ★loop 6 tog, rib 2, rep from ★ to last 4 [4: 5: 5: 6: 6: 7: 7] sts, (loop 6 tog) 0 [0: 0: 0: 0: 0: 1: 1] times, rib 4 [4: 5: 5: 6: 6: 1: 1].

Work 1 row.

Last 8 rows form smocked rib.

Cont in smocked rib for a further 5 rows, ending with **WS** facing for next row.

Row 14 (WS): Rib 2 [2: 3: 3: 4: 4: 5: 5], (work 2 tog, rib 2) 4 times, rib 14, (rib 2, work 2 tog) 4 times, rib to end.

42 [42: 44: 44: 46: 46: 48: 48] sts.

Change to 9mm (US 13) needles.

Keeping centre 14 sts correct in smocked rib as set, now work cable patt over edge sts as folls:

Row 1 (RS): P6 [6: 7: 7: 8: 8: 9: 9], K4, P4, rib 14, P4, K4, P to end.

Row 2: K6 [6: 7: 7: 8: 8: 9: 9], P4, K4, rib 14, K4, P4, K to end.

Row 3: P6 [6: 7: 7: 8: 8: 9: 9], C4B, P4, rib 14, P4, C4F, P to end.

Row 4: As row 2.

These 4 rows form patt.

Cont in patt, shaping sides by inc 1 st at each end of next [next: next: next: 3rd: next: next: next] and every foll 6th [6th: 8th: 6th: 8th: 6th: 8th: 6th] row to 46 [54: 56: 54: 58: 54: 60: 58] sts, then on every foll 8th [8th: –: 8th: –: 8th: –: 8th] row until there are 54 [56: –: 58: –:

60: –: 62] sts, taking inc sts into rev st st.

Cont straight until sleeve meas 44 [44: 45: 45: 46: 46: 45: 45] cm, ending with RS facing for next row.

Shape raglan

Cast off 3 sts at beg of next 2 rows.

48 [50: 50: 52: 52: 54: 54: 56] sts.

Dec 1 st at each end of next and 2 foll 4th rows, then on every foll alt row until 22 sts rem.

Work 1 row, ending with RS facing for next row.

Left sleeve only

Dec 1 st at each end of next row, then cast off 6 sts at beg of foll row.

14 sts.

Dec 1 st at beg of next row, then cast off 7 sts at beg of foll row.

Right sleeve only

Cast off 7 sts at beg and dec 1 st at end of next row.

14 sts.

Work 1 row.

Rep last 2 rows once more.

Both sleeves

Cast off rem 6 sts.

MAKING UP

Press as described on the information page.

Join both front and right back raglan seams using back stitch, or mattress stitch if preferred.

Collar

With RS facing and using 8mm (US 11) needles, pick up and knit 17 [17: 17: 17: 15: 15: 15: 15] sts from left sleeve, and 6 sts down left side of neck, patt 24 [24: 24: 24: 26: 26: 26: 26] sts from front holder, pick up and K 6 sts up right side of neck, and 17 [17: 17: 17: 15: 15: 15: 15] sts from right sleeve, then patt 34 [34: 34: 34: 36: 36: 36: 36] sts from back holder.

104 sts.

Keeping rib correct as set by back neck sts, work in rib for 1 row, ending with RS facing for next row.

Now keeping **smocked** rib correct as set by centre front neck sts, work in smocked rib for 13 rows, ending with **WS** facing for next row.

Cast off in rib (on **WS**).

See information page for finishing instructions.

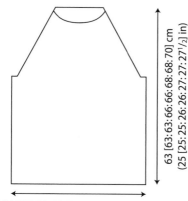

45.5 [47.5: 51: 52.5: 56.5: 58: 62: 65.5] cm
(18 [18½: 20: 20½: 22: 23: 24½: 26] in)

63 [63: 63: 66: 66: 66: 68: 68: 70] cm
(25 [25: 25: 26: 26: 27: 27: 27½] in)

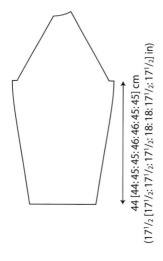

44 [44: 45: 45: 46: 46: 45: 45] cm
(17½ [17½: 17½: 17½: 18: 18: 17½: 17½] in)

HOLLY

by MARIE WALLIN

Main image page 11

SIZE

8	10	12	14	16	18	
To fit bust						
82	87	92	97	102	107	cm
32	34	36	38	40	42	in

YARN

Rowan Big Wool Fusion

7	8	8	8	9	9	x 100gm

(photographed in Willow 008)

NEEDLES

1 pair 9mm (no 00) (US 13) needles
1 pair 10mm (no 000) (US 15) needles

TENSION

9 sts and 12 rows to 10 cm measured over
stocking stitch using 10mm (US 15) needles.

SPECIAL ABBREVIATION

MB = K into front, back and front again of
next st, turn and K3, turn and P3, lift 2nd and
3rd sts on right needle over first st and off right
needle. Do NOT place bobbles on edge sts of
rows as these will interfere with sewing up.

BACK and FRONT (both alike)
Using 9mm (US 13) needles cast on 41 [43:
45: 47: 51: 53] sts.
Beg with a P row, work in st st for 5 rows,
ending with RS facing for next row.
Change to 10mm (US 15) needles.
Beg and ending rows as indicated and repeating
the 32 row patt repeat throughout, cont in patt
from chart for body as folls:
Dec 1 st at each end of 11th and foll 6th row.
37 [39: 41: 43: 47: 49] sts.

Work 9 rows, ending with RS facing for
next row.
Inc 1 st at each end of next and foll 8th row.
41 [43: 45: 47: 51: 53] sts.
Cont straight until work meas 39 [39: 38:
41: 40: 42] cm, ending with RS facing for
next row.

Shape armholes

Keeping patt correct, cast off 3 sts at beg of
next 2 rows.
35 [37: 39: 41: 45: 47] sts.
Dec 1 st at each end of next 1 [1: 1: 1: 3: 3]
rows, then on foll 0 [1: 2: 2: 2: 2] alt rows.
33 [33: 33: 35: 35: 37] sts.
Cont straight until armhole meas 21 [21: 22:
22: 23: 23] cm, ending with RS facing for
next row.

Shape shoulders

Keeping patt correct, cast off 4 sts at beg of
next 2 rows, then 4 [4: 4: 5: 4: 5] sts at beg of
foll 2 rows.
Cont in patt on rem 17 [17: 17: 17: 19: 19] sts
(for funnel collar extension) for approx 10 cm,
ending after chart row 8, 16, 24 or 32 and with
RS facing for next row.
Cast off purlwise (on RS).

SLEEVES

Using 9mm (US 13) needles cast on 29 [29:
29: 29: 31: 31] sts.
Beg with a P row, work in st st for 5 rows,
ending with RS facing for next row.
Change to 10mm (US 15) needles.
Beg and ending rows as indicated and repeating
the 32 row patt repeat throughout, cont in patt
from chart for sleeve, shaping sides by dec 1 st

at each end of 7th and foll 8th row.
25 [25: 25: 25: 27: 27] sts.
Work 11 rows, ending with RS facing for
next row.
Inc 1 st at each end of next and every foll

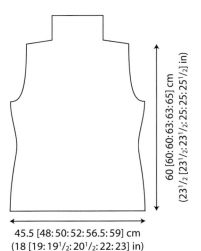

60 [60: 60: 63: 63: 65] cm
(23¹/₂ [23¹/₂: 23¹/₂: 25: 25: 25¹/₂] in)

45.5 [48: 50: 52: 56.5: 59] cm
(18 [19: 19¹/₂: 20¹/₂: 22: 23] in)

45 [45: 46: 46: 47: 47] cm
(17¹/₂ [17¹/₂: 18: 18: 18¹/₂: 18¹/₂] in)

4th row to 29 [29: 33: 33: 33: 33] sts, then on
every foll 6th row until there are 33 [33: 35:
35: 37: 37] sts, taking inc sts into patt.
Cont straight until sleeve meas 45 [45: 46:
46: 47: 47] cm, ending with RS facing for
next row.

Shape top
Keeping patt correct, cast off 3 sts at beg of
next 2 rows.
27 [27: 29: 29: 31: 31] sts.
Dec 1 st at each end of next and every foll 4th
row to 21 [21: 23: 23: 25: 25] sts, then on every
foll alt row until 17 sts rem, then on foll row,
ending with RS facing for next row.
Cast off rem 15 sts.

MAKING UP
Press as described on the information page.
Join both shoulder and funnel neck seams
using back stitch, or mattress stitch if preferred.
See information page for finishing instructions,
setting in sleeves using the set-in method.

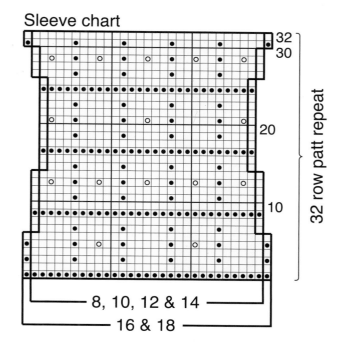

Sleeve chart

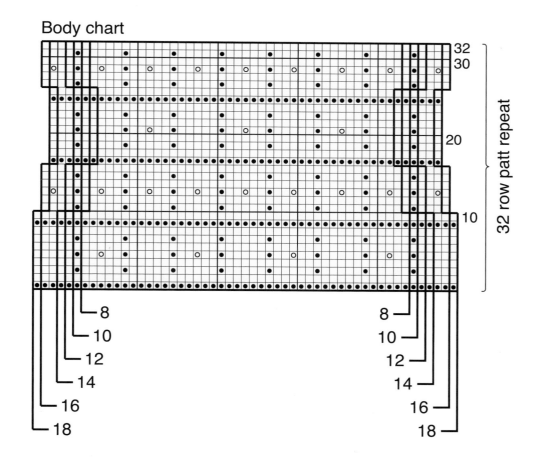

Body chart

Key

☐ K on RS,
P on WS

▪ P on RS,
K on WS

◉ MB

BLYTHE

by MARIE WALLIN

Main image page 2

SIZE

8	10	12	14	16	
To fit bust					
82	87	92	97	102	cm
32	34	36	38	40	in

YARN

Rowan Little Big Wool

A Amethyst 504

3	3	3	4	4	x 50gm

B Onyx 501

2	2	2	2	2	x 50gm

NEEDLES

1 pair 8mm (no 0) (US 11) needles
1 pair 9mm (no 00) (US 13) needles

TENSION

11 sts and 15 rows to 10 cm measured over stocking stitch using 9mm (US 13) needles.

BACK

Using 8mm (US 11) needles and yarn A cast on 45 [47: 49: 53: 57] sts.
Row 1 (RS): K0 [1: 2: 0: 0], P3 [3: 3: 1: 3], ★K3, P3, rep from ★ to last 0 [1: 2: 4: 0] sts, K0 [1: 2: 3: 0], P0 [0: 0: 1: 0].
Row 2: P0 [1: 2: 0: 0], K3 [3: 3: 1: 3], ★P3, K3, rep from ★ to last 0 [1: 2: 4: 0] sts, P0 [1: 2: 3: 0], K0 [0: 0: 1: 0].
These 2 rows form rib.
Work in rib for a further 10 rows, dec 1 st at end of last row and ending with RS facing for next row. 44 [46: 48: 52: 56] sts.
Break off yarn A and join in yarn B.
Change to 9mm (US 13) needles.
Beg with a K row, work in st st until back meas 28 [28: 27: 30: 29] cm, ending with RS facing

for next row.
Shape armholes
Cast off 2 sts at beg of next 2 rows.
40 [42: 44: 48: 52] sts.
Dec 1 st at each end of next 1 [3: 3: 5: 5] rows, then on foll 2 [1: 1: 1: 2] alt rows.
34 [34: 36: 36: 38] sts.
Cont straight until armhole meas 20 [20: 21: 21: 22] cm, end with RS facing for next row.
Shape back neck
Next row (RS): K8 [8: 9: 8: 9] and turn, leaving rem sts on a holder.
Work each side of neck separately.
Cast off 3 sts at beg of next row. 5 [5: 6: 5: 6] sts.
Work 2 rows, end with RS facing for next row.
Shape shoulder
Cast off rem 5 [5: 6: 5: 6] sts.
With RS facing, rejoin yarn to rem sts, cast off centre 18 [18: 18: 20: 20] sts, K to end.
Complete to match first side, reversing shapings.

FRONT

Work as given for back until 2 rows less have been worked than on back to beg of armhole shaping, ending with RS facing for next row.
Shape neck
Next row (RS): K18 [19: 20: 21: 23] and turn, leaving rem sts on a holder.
Work each side of neck separately.
Dec 1 st at neck edge of next row, ending with RS facing for next row. 17 [18: 19: 20: 22] sts.
Shape armhole
Cast off 2 sts at beg and dec 1 st at end of next row. 14 [15: 16: 17: 19] sts.
Work 1 row.
Dec 1 st at armhole edge of next 1 [3: 3: 5: 5]

rows, then on foll 2 [1: 1: 1: 2] alt rows **and at same time** dec 1 st at neck edge of next and foll 2 alt rows, then on 3 foll 4th rows.
5 [5: 6: 5: 6] sts.
Cont straight until front matches back to shoulder cast-off, ending with RS facing for next row.
Shape shoulder
Cast off rem 5 [5: 6: 5: 6] sts.
With RS facing, rejoin yarn to rem sts, cast off centre 8 [8: 8: 10: 10] sts, K to end.
Complete to match first side, reversing shapings.

MAKING UP
Press as described on the information page.
Join right shoulder seam using back stitch, or mattress stitch if preferred.
Neck band
With RS facing, using 8mm (US 11) needles and yarn A, pick up and knit 33 sts down left side of front neck, 8 [8: 8: 10: 10] sts from front, 33 sts up right side of front neck, 6 sts

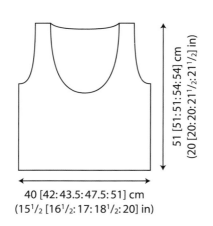

51 [51: 51: 54: 54] cm
(20 [20: 20: 21½: 21½] in)

40 [42: 43.5: 47.5: 51] cm
(15½ [16½: 17: 18½: 20] in)

down right side of back neck, 17 [17: 17: 21: 21] sts from back, then 6 sts up left side of back neck. 103 [103: 103: 109: 109] sts.
Row 1 (WS): P2, ★K3, P3, rep from ★ to last 5 sts, K3, P2.
Row 2: K2, ★P3, K3, rep from ★ to last 5 sts, P3, K2.

These 2 rows form rib.
Work in rib for a further 2 rows, ending with **WS** facing for next row.
Cast off in rib (on **WS**).
Join left shoulder and neck band seam.
Armhole borders (both alike)
With RS facing, using 8mm (US 11) needles

and yarn A, pick up and knit 55 [55: 55: 61: 61] sts all round armhole edge.
Work in rib as given for neck band for 4 rows, ending with **WS** facing for next row.
Cast off in rib (on **WS**).
See information page for finishing instructions.

RHIANNON
by MARIE WALLIN

Main image page 6

YARN
Rowan Little Big Wool
5 x 50gm
(photographed in Aquamarine 502)

NEEDLES
8.00mm (no 0) (US L11) crochet hook

TENSION
2 patt repeats, both in sts and rows, to 15 cm measured over pattern using 8.00mm (US L11) crochet hook.

FINISHED SIZE
Completed scarf measures 23 cm (9 in) wide and 140 cm (55 in) long.

UK CROCHET ABBREVIATIONS
ch = chain; **sp** = space; **tr** = treble.

US CROCHET ABBREVIATIONS
ch = chain; **sp** = space; **tr** = double.

SCARF
Using 8.00mm (US L11) crochet hook make 27 ch.
Foundation row (RS): 1 tr into 4th ch from hook, ★1 ch, miss 2 ch, (1 tr, 3 ch and 1 tr) into next ch, 1 ch, miss 2 ch★★, 1 tr into each of next 3 ch, rep from ★ to end, ending last rep at ★★, 1 tr into each of last 2 ch, turn. 3 patt reps.
Cont in patt as folls:
Row 1: 4 ch (counts as 1 tr and 1 ch), miss (2 tr, 1 ch and 1 tr) at end of previous row, ★7 tr into next ch sp, 1 ch, miss (1 tr, 1 ch and 1 tr)★★, 1 tr into next tr, 1 ch, miss (1 tr, 1 ch and 1 tr), rep from ★ to end, ending last rep at ★★, 1 tr into top of 3 ch at beg of previous row, turn.
Row 2: 4 ch (counts as 1 tr and 1 ch), 1 tr into tr at base of 4 ch, ★1 ch, miss (1 ch and 2 tr), 1 tr into each of next 3 tr, 1 ch, miss (2 tr and 1 ch)★★, (1 tr, 3 ch and 1 tr) into next tr, rep from ★ to end, ending last rep at ★★, (1 tr, 1 ch and 1 tr) into 3rd of 4 ch at beg of previous

row, turn.
Row 3: 3 ch (counts as first tr), miss tr at base of 3 ch, 3 tr into first ch sp, ★1 ch, miss (1 tr, 1 ch and 1 tr), 1 tr into next tr, 1 ch, miss (1 tr, 1 ch and 1 tr)★★, 7 tr into next ch sp, rep from ★ to end, ending last rep at ★★, 3 tr into last ch sp, 1 tr into 3rd of 4 ch at beg of previous row, turn.
Row 4: 3 ch (counts as first tr), miss tr at base of 3 ch, 1 tr into next tr, ★1 ch, miss (2 tr and 1 ch), (1 tr, 3 ch and 1 tr) into next tr, 1 ch, miss (1 ch and 2 tr)★★, 1 tr into each of next 3 tr, rep from ★ to end, ending last rep at ★★, 1 tr into next tr, 1 tr into top of 3 ch at beg of previous row, turn.
These 4 rows form patt.
Cont in patt until scarf meas approx 140 cm, ending with patt row 4.
Fasten off.

MAKING UP
Press as described on the information page.

REUBEN

by MARITIN STOREY

Main image page 10

SIZE

	S	M	L	XL	XXL	
To fit chest						
	102	107	112	117	122	cm
	40	42	44	46	48	in

YARN

Rowan Big Wool Fusion

9	9	10	11	12	x 100gm

(photographed in Soot 006)

NEEDLES

1 pair 10mm (no 000) (US 15) needles
1 pair 12mm (US 17) needles
10mm (no 000) (US 15) circular needle
12mm (US 17) circular needle
Cable needle

TENSION

8 sts and 12 rows to 10 cm measured over stocking stitch using 12mm (US 17) needles.

Pattern note: The number of sts varies whilst working the chart. All st counts given assume there are 34 sts in chart **at all times**.

SPECIAL ABBREVIATIONS

Cr4R = slip next st onto cable needle and leave at back of work, K3, then P1 from cable needle; **Cr4L** = slip next 3 sts onto cable needle and leave at front of work, P1, then K3 from cable needle; **Cr5R** = slip next 2 sts onto cable needle and leave at back of work, K3, then P2 from cable needle; **Cr5L** = slip next 3 sts onto cable needle and leave at front of work, P2, then K3 from cable needle; **C6B** = slip next 3 sts onto cable needle and leave at back of work, K3, then K3 from cable needle; **C6F** = slip next 3 sts onto cable needle and leave at front of work, K3, then K3 from cable needle; **C7B** = slip next 4 sts onto cable needle and leave at back of work, K3, slip last st on cable needle back onto left needle and P this st, then K3 from cable needle; **dec7** = with yarn at front of work slip next 4 sts onto right needle, *lift 2nd st on right needle over first st and off right needle, slip first st on right needle back onto left needle, lift 2nd st on left needle over first st and off left needle, slip first st on left needle back onto right needle, rep from * twice more, slip first st on right needle back onto left needle and K this st; **inc2K** = (K1 tbl, K1) into next st, insert left needle point behind vertical strand that runs downwards from between 2 sts just made and K1 tbl into this loop; **inc2P** = (P1, yrn, P1) all into next st.

BACK

Using 10mm (US 15) needles cast on 44 [46: 48: 52: 54] sts.
Row 1 (RS): K1 [0: 0: 1: 0], P2 [0: 1: 2: 0], *K2, P2, rep from * to last 1 [2: 3: 1: 2] sts, K1 [2: 2: 1: 2], P0 [0: 1: 0: 0].
Row 2: P1 [0: 0: 1: 0], K2 [0: 1: 2: 0], *P2, K2, rep from * to last 1 [2: 3: 1: 2] sts, P1 [2: 2: 1: 2], K0 [0: 1: 0: 0].
These 2 rows form rib.
Work in rib for a further 8 rows, ending with RS facing for next row.
Change to 12mm (US 17) needles.
Beg with a K row, work in st st until back meas 41 [42: 41: 42: 41] cm, ending with RS facing for next row.

Shape armholes

Cast off 3 sts at beg of next 2 rows.
38 [40: 42: 46: 48] sts.
Dec 1 st at each end of next 3 [3: 2: 3: 2] rows.
32 [34: 38: 40: 44] sts.
Cont straight until armhole meas 23 [24: 25: 26: 27] cm, ending with RS facing for next row.

Shape shoulders and back neck

Next row (RS): Cast off 4 [5: 6: 6: 7] sts, K until there are 8 [8: 9: 10: 10] sts on right needle and turn, leaving rem sts on a holder.
Work each side of neck separately.
Cast off 3 sts at beg of next row.
Cast off rem 5 [5: 6: 7: 7] sts.
With RS facing, rejoin yarn to rem sts, cast off centre 8 [8: 8: 8: 10] sts, K to end.
Complete to match first side, reversing shapings.

FRONT

Using 10mm (US 15) needles cast on 44 [46: 48: 52: 54] sts.
Work in rib as given for back for 9 rows, ending with **WS** facing for next row.
Row 10 (WS): Rib 12 [13: 14: 16: 17], M1, rib 8, M1, rib 1, M1, rib 2, M1, rib 1, M1, rib 8, M1, rib to end.
50 [52: 54: 58: 60] sts.
Change to 12mm (US 17) needles.

Place chart

Row 1 (RS): K8 [9: 10: 12: 13], work next 34 sts as row 1 of chart, K to end.
Row 2: P8 [9: 10: 12: 13], work next 34 sts as row 2 of chart, P to end.

These 2 rows set the sts – central chart with st st at either side.

Cont as set until front matches back to beg of armhole shaping, ending with RS facing for next row.

Shape armholes

Keeping patt correct, cast off 3 sts at beg of next 2 rows.

44 [46: 48: 52: 54] sts.

Dec 1 st at each end of next 3 [3: 2: 3: 2] rows.

38 [40: 44: 46: 50] sts.

Cont straight until 8 rows less have been worked than on back to beg of shoulder shaping, ending with RS facing for next row.

Shape neck

Next row (RS): Patt 15 [16: 18: 19: 20] sts and turn, leaving rem sts on a holder.

Work each side of neck separately.

Keeping patt correct, dec 1 st at neck edge of next 4 rows, then on foll alt row.

10 [11: 13: 14: 15] sts.

Work 1 row, ending with RS facing for next row.

Shape shoulder

Cast off 4 [5: 6: 6: 7] sts at beg of next row.

Work 1 row.

Cast off rem 6 [6: 7: 8: 8] sts.

With RS facing, rejoin yarn to rem sts, cast off centre 8 [8: 8: 8: 10] sts, patt to end.

Complete to match first side, reversing shapings.

SLEEVES

Using 10mm (US 15) needles cast on 20 [22: 22: 24: 24] sts.

Row 1 (RS): K1 [0: 0: 0: 0], P2 [0: 0: 1: 1], ★K2, P2, rep from ★ to last 1 [2: 2: 3: 3] sts, K1 [2: 2: 2: 2], P0 [0: 0: 1: 1].

Row 2: P1 [0: 0: 0: 0], K2 [0: 0: 1: 1], ★P2, K2, rep from ★ to last 1 [2: 2: 3: 3] sts, P1 [2: 2: 2: 2], K0 [0: 0: 1: 1].

These 2 rows form rib.

Work in rib for a further 8 rows, ending with RS facing for next row.

Change to 12mm (US 17) needles.

Beg with a K row, work in st st, shaping sides by inc 1 st at each end of next and every foll 10th [12th: 10th: 10th: 10th] row to 26 [32: 32: 28: 38] sts, then on every foll 12th [–: 12th: 12th: –] row until there are 30 [–: 34: 36: –] sts.

Cont straight until sleeve meas 50 [53: 56: 61: 64] cm, ending with RS facing for next row.

Shape top

Cast off 3 sts at beg of next 2 rows.

24 [26: 28: 30: 32] sts.

Dec 1 st at each end of next and 2 foll 4th rows, then on every foll alt row to 14 sts, then on foll 3 rows, ending with RS facing for next row.

Cast off rem 8 sts.

MAKING UP

Press as described on the information page.

Join both shoulder seams using back stitch, or mattress stitch if preferred.

Collar

With RS facing and using 10mm (US 15) circular needle, pick up and knit 11 sts down left side of neck, 8 [8: 8: 8: 10] sts from front, 11 sts up right side of neck, then 14 [14: 14: 14: 16] sts from back.

44 [44: 44: 44: 48] sts.

Round 1 (RS): ★K2, P2, rep from ★ to end.

This round forms rib.

Cont in rib until collar meas 9 cm.

Change to 12mm (US 17) circular needle.

Cont in rib until collar meas 19 cm.

Cast off in rib.

See information page for finishing instructions, setting in sleeves using the set-in method.

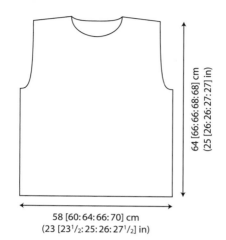

64 [66: 66: 68: 68] cm
(25 [26: 26: 27: 27] in)

58 [60: 64: 66: 70] cm
(23 [23½: 25: 26: 27½] in)

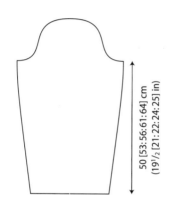

50 [53: 56: 61: 64] cm
(19½ [21: 22: 24: 25] in)

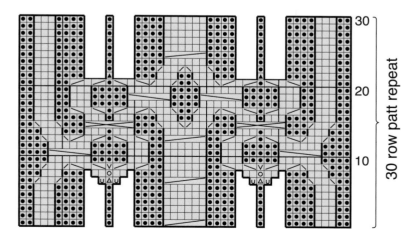

30 row patt repeat

Key

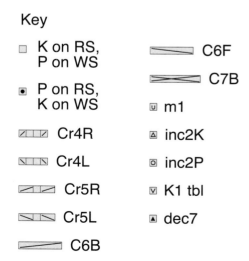

☐ K on RS, P on WS

⊡ P on RS, K on WS

Cr4R

Cr4L

Cr5R

Cr5L

C6B

C6F

C7B

m1

inc2K

inc2P

K1 tbl

dec7

39

HERMIONE

by MARIE WALLIN

Main image page 18

SIZE

8	10	12	14	16	18	
To fit bust						
82	87	92	97	102	107	cm
32	34	36	38	40	42	in

YARN

Rowan Biggy Print

14	15	16	16	17	19	x 100gm

(photographed in Jewel 264)

NEEDLES

1 pair 10mm (no 000) (US 15) needles
1 pair 12mm (US 17) needles
10mm (no 000) (US 15) circular needle

TENSION

7 sts and 10 rows to 10 cm measured over stocking stitch using 12mm (US 17) needles.

SPECIAL ABBREVIATION

loop 1 = insert right needle into next st, bring yarn to front (WS) of work between needle points and wrap yarn twice round left thumb, take yarn back to back (RS) of work between needle points, bring the 2 loops now on right needle through st on left needle and let loop fall off left thumb and over needles onto RS of work – on next row K tog these 2 loops.

BACK

Using 12mm (US 17) needles cast on 33 [35: 37: 39: 41: 43] sts.
Row 1 (RS): Knit.
Row 2: K2 [1: 2: 1: 2: 1], *loop 1, K1, rep from * to last 1 [0: 1: 0: 1: 0] st, K1 [0: 1: 0: 1: 0].
Row 3: Knit.

Row 4: K1 [2: 1: 2: 1: 2], *loop 1, K1, rep from * to last 0 [1: 0: 1: 0: 1] st, K0 [1: 0: 1: 0: 1].
Rows 5 and 6: As rows 1 and 2.
Beg with a K row, work in st st, shaping side seams by dec 1 st at each end of 5th and foll 4th row. 29 [31: 33: 35: 37: 39] sts.
Work 5 rows, ending with RS facing for next row.
Inc 1 st at each end of next and foll 8th row. 33 [35: 37: 39: 41: 43] sts.
Cont straight until back meas 34 [34: 33: 36: 35: 37] cm, ending with RS facing for next row.

Shape armholes

Cast off 3 sts at beg of next 2 rows. 27 [29: 31: 33: 35: 37] sts.
Dec 1 st at each end of next and foll 0 [1: 1: 2: 2: 3] alt rows.
25 [25: 27: 27: 29: 29] sts.
Cont straight until armhole meas 21 [21: 22: 22: 23: 23] cm, ending with RS facing for next row.

Shape back neck

Next row (RS): K8 [8: 9: 9: 9: 9] and turn, leaving rem sts on a holder.
Work each side of neck separately.
Cast off 3 sts at beg of next row.

Shape shoulder

Cast off rem 5 [5: 6: 6: 6: 6] sts.
With RS facing, rejoin yarn to rem sts, cast off centre 9 [9: 9: 9: 11: 11] sts, K to end.
Complete to match first side, reversing shapings.

LEFT FRONT

Using 12mm (US 17) needles cast on 14 [15:

16: 17: 18: 19] sts.
Row 1 (RS): Knit.
Row 2: K1, *loop 1, K1, rep from * to last 1 [0: 1: 0: 1: 0] st, K1 [0: 1: 0: 1: 0].
Row 3: Knit.
Row 4: K2, *loop 1, K1, rep from * to last 0 [1: 0: 1: 0: 1] st, K0 [1: 0: 1: 0: 1].
Rows 5 and 6: As rows 1 and 2.
Beg with a K row, work in st st, shaping side seam by dec 1 st at beg of 5th and foll 4th row.
12 [13: 14: 15: 16: 17] sts.
Work 5 rows, ending with RS facing for next row.
Inc 1 st at beg of next and foll 8th row.
14 [15: 16: 17: 18: 19] sts.
Cont straight until 2 rows less have been worked than on back to beg of armhole shaping, ending with RS facing for next row.

Shape front slope

Dec 1 st at end of next row.
13 [14: 15: 16: 17: 18] sts.
Work 1 row, ending with RS facing for next row.

Shape armhole

Cast off 3 sts at beg of next row.
10 [11: 12: 13: 14: 15] sts.
Work 1 row.
Dec 1 st at armhole edge of next and foll 0 [1: 1: 2: 2: 3] alt rows **and at same time** dec 1 st at front slope edge of next and foll 0 [0: 0: 4th: 4th: 4th] row.
8 [8: 9: 8: 9: 9] sts.
Dec 1 st at front slope edge **only** of 4th [2nd: 2nd: 4th: 4th: 2nd] and every foll 4th [4th: 4th: 6th: 4th: 4th] row to 5 [5: 7: 6: 6: 6] sts, then on foll 0 [0: 6th: 0: 0: 0] row.
5 [5: 6: 6: 6: 6] sts.

Cont straight until left front matches back to shoulder cast-off, ending with RS facing for next row.

Shape shoulder
Cast off rem 5 [5: 6: 6: 6: 6] sts.

RIGHT FRONT
Using 12mm (US 17) needles cast on 14 [15: 16: 17: 18: 19] sts.
Row 1 (RS): Knit.
Row 2: K2 [1: 2: 1: 2: 1], ⋆loop 1, K1, rep from ⋆ to end.
Row 3: Knit.
Row 4: K1 [2: 1: 2: 1: 2], ⋆loop 1, K1, rep from ⋆ to last st, K1.
Rows 5 and 6: As rows 1 and 2.
Beg with a K row, work in st st, shaping side seam by dec 1 st at end of 5th and foll 4th row.
12 [13: 14: 15: 16: 17] sts.
Complete to match left front, reversing shapings.

SLEEVES
Using 10mm (US 15) needles cast on 19 [19: 21: 21: 23: 23] sts.
Row 1 (RS): Knit.
Row 2: K1, ⋆loop 1, K1, rep from ⋆ to end.
Row 3: Knit.
Row 4: K2, ⋆loop 1, K1, rep from ⋆ to last st, K1.
Rows 5 and 6: As rows 1 and 2.
Change to 12mm (US 17) needles.
Beg with a K row, work in st st, shaping sides by inc 1 st at each end of 5th and every foll 10th row to 27 [27: 29: 29: 29: 29] sts, then on every foll – [-: -: -: 12th: 12th] row until there

are – [-: -: -: 31: 31] sts.
Cont straight until sleeve meas 44 [44: 45: 45: 46: 46] cm, ending with RS facing for next row.
Shape top
Cast off 3 sts at beg of next 2 rows.
21 [21: 23: 23: 25: 25] sts.
Dec 1 st at each end of next and every foll 4th row to 15 [15: 17: 17: 19: 19] sts, then on foll 1 [1: 2: 2: 3: 3] alt rows, then on foll row, ending with RS facing for next row.
Cast off rem 11 sts.

MAKING UP
Press as described on the information page.
Join both shoulder seams using back stitch, or mattress stitch if preferred.
Front band
With RS facing and using 10mm (US 15) circular needle, beg and ending at cast-on edges, pick up and knit 25 [25: 24: 26: 26: 27] sts up right front opening edge to beg of front slope shaping, 19 [19: 20: 20: 21: 21] sts up right front slope, 15 [15: 15: 15: 17: 17] sts from back, 19 [19: 20: 20: 21: 21] sts down left front slope to beg of front slope shaping, then 25 [25: 24: 26: 26: 27] sts down left front opening edge.
103 [103: 103: 107: 111: 113] sts.
Row 1 (WS): K1, ⋆loop 1, K1, rep from ⋆ to end.
Row 2: Knit.
Row 3: K2, ⋆loop 1, K1, rep from ⋆ to last st, K1.
Row 4: Knit.
Cast off in patt (on **WS**), making loop on 2nd

and every foll alt st before casting off.
See information page for finishing instructions, setting in sleeves using the set-in method.
Make 2 twisted cords, each 30 cm long, and knot one end. Attach other end to front opening edge level with beg of front slope shaping.

57 [57: 57: 60: 60: 62] cm
(22¹/₂ [22¹/₂: 22¹/₂: 23¹/₂: 23¹/₂: 24¹/₂] in)

47 [50: 53: 55.5: 58.5: 61.5] cm
(18¹/₂ [19¹/₂: 21: 22: 23: 24] in)

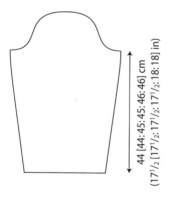

44 [44: 45: 45: 46: 46] cm
(17¹/₂ [17¹/₂: 17¹/₂: 17¹/₂: 18: 18] in)

SETH

by MARIE WALLIN

Main image page 15

SIZE

	S	M	L	XL	XXL	
To fit chest						
	102	107	112	117	122	cm
	40	42	44	46	48	in

YARN

Rowan Little Big Wool

A Topaz	509					
	11	11	12	13	14	x 50gm
B Moonstone	507					
	2	2	3	3	3	x 50gm

NEEDLES

1 pair 8mm (no 0) (US 11) needles
1 pair 9mm (no 00) (US 13) needles

FASTENINGS – 5 x 00326 buttons and
7 large press fasteners

TENSION

11 sts and 15 rows to 10 cm measured over
stocking stitch using 9mm (US 13) needles.

BACK

Using 9mm (US 13) needles and yarn A cast
on 64 [68: 72: 74: 78] sts.
Beg with a K row, work in st st until back meas
34 [35: 34: 35: 34] cm, ending with RS facing
for next row.
Break off yarn A and join in yarn B.
Next row (RS): Knit.
Beg with a **K** row, work in rev st st as folls:
Work 1 row, ending with RS facing for
next row.
Shape armholes
Cast off 5 sts at beg of next 2 rows.
54 [58: 62: 64: 68] sts.

Dec 1 st at each end of next 3 [3: 3: 1: 1] rows,
then on foll 1 [1: 1: 2: 1] alt rows.
46 [50: 54: 58: 64] sts.
Work 11 [11: 11: 11: 13] rows, ending with
RS facing for next row.
Break off yarn B and join in yarn A.
Beg with a K row, cont in st st until armhole
meas 24 [25: 26: 27: 28] cm, ending with RS
facing for next row.
Shape shoulders and back neck
Next row (RS): Cast off 6 [7: 8: 9: 10] sts,
K until there are 10 [11: 11: 12: 14] sts on right
needle and turn, leaving rem sts on a holder.
Work each side of neck separately.
Cast off 3 sts at beg of next row.
Cast off rem 7 [8: 8: 9: 11] sts.
With RS facing, rejoin yarn to rem sts, cast off
centre 14 [14: 16: 16: 16] sts, K to end.
Complete to match first side, reversing
shapings.

LEFT FRONT
Using 9mm (US 13) needles and yarn A cast
on 30 [32: 34: 35: 37] sts.
Beg with a K row, work in st st until left front
meas 34 [35: 34: 35: 34] cm, ending with RS
facing for next row.
Break off yarn A and join in yarn B.
Next row (RS): Knit.
Beg with a **K** row, work in rev st st as folls:
Work 1 row, ending with RS facing for
next row.
Shape armhole
Cast off 5 sts at beg of next row.
25 [27: 29: 30: 32] sts.
Work 1 row.
Dec 1 st at armhole edge of next 3 [3: 3: 1: 1]

rows, then on foll 1 [1: 1: 2: 1] alt rows.
21 [23: 25: 27: 30] sts.
Work 11 [11: 11: 11: 13] rows, ending with RS
facing for next row.
Break off yarn B and join in yarn A.
Beg with a K row, cont in st st until 11 [11: 13:
13: 13] rows less have been worked than on
back to beg of shoulder shaping, ending with
WS facing for next row.
Shape neck
Cast off 3 sts at beg of next row.
18 [20: 22: 24: 27] sts.
Dec 1 st at neck edge of next 3 rows, then on
foll 2 [2: 3: 3: 3] alt rows.
13 [15: 16: 18: 21] sts.
Work 3 rows, ending with RS facing for
next row.
Shape shoulder
Cast off 6 [7: 8: 9: 10] sts at beg of next row.
Work 1 row.
Cast off rem 7 [8: 8: 9: 11] sts.

RIGHT FRONT
Work to match left front, reversing shapings.

SLEEVES
Using 9mm (US 13) needles and yarn A cast
on 27 [29: 31: 31: 33] sts.
Beg with a K row, work in st st, shaping sides by
inc 1 st at each end of 5th and every foll 6th row
to 37 [37: 35: 41: 39] sts, then on every foll 8th
row until there are 47 [49: 51: 53: 55] sts.
Cont straight until sleeve meas 50 [52: 54:
56: 58] cm, ending with RS facing for next
row.
Break off yarn A and join in yarn B.
Next row (RS): Knit.

Beg with a **K** row, work in rev st st as folls:
Work 1 row, ending with RS facing for
next row.

Shape top
Cast off 5 sts at beg of next 2 rows.
37 [39: 41: 43: 45] sts.
Dec 1 st at each end of next and 3 foll
4th rows.
29 [31: 33: 35: 37] sts.
Work 3 rows, ending with RS facing for
next row.
Break off yarn B and join in yarn A.
Beg with a K row, cont in st st, dec 1 st at each
end of next and every foll alt row to 25 sts,
then on foll 3 rows, ending with RS facing for
next row.
Cast off rem 19 sts.

MAKING UP
Press as described on the information page.
Join both shoulder seams using back stitch, or
mattress stitch if preferred.

Collar
Using 8mm (US 11) needles and yarn A cast
on 15 sts.
Row 1 (RS): K2, *P1, K1, rep from * to last
st, K1.
Row 2: K1, *P1, K1, rep from * to end.
These 2 rows form rib.
Cont in rib until collar, when slightly
stretched, fits around entire neck edge, between
front opening edges and ending with RS
facing for next row.
Cast off in rib.
Slip stitch collar in place.

Front bands (both alike)
Using 8mm (US 11) needles and yarn A cast
on 9 sts.
Work in rib as given for collar until band,
when slightly stretched, fits front opening edge,
from cast-on edge to top of collar and ending
with RS facing for next row.
Cast off in rib.
Slip stitch bands in place. Join side seams.

Hem band
Using 8mm (US 11) needles and yarn A cast
on 9 sts.

Work in rib as given for collar until hem band,
when slightly stretched, fits around entire cast-
on edge, beg at right front opening edge,
ending at right front opening edge and ending
with RS facing for next row.
Next row (RS): Work 2 tog, rib 2, yfwd (to
make a buttonhole), K2tog, rib 1, work 2 tog.
7 sts.
Work 1 row.
Next row (RS): Work 2 tog, rib to last 2 sts,
work 2 tog.
Work 1 row.
Rep last 2 rows once more. 3 sts.
Next row (RS): sl 1, K2tog, psso and
fasten off.
Slip stitch band in place.

Cuff bands (both alike)
Using 8mm (US 11) needles and yarn A cast
on 9 sts.
Work in rib as given for collar until band,
when slightly stretched, fits along entire cast-on
edge of sleeve, ending with RS facing for
next row.
Cast off in rib.
Slip stitch bands in place.

Epaulettes (make 2)
Using 8mm (US 11) needles and yarn A cast
on 9 sts.
Work in rib as given for collar until epaulette
meas 12 cm, ending with **WS** facing for next
row.
Cast off in rib (on **WS**).
Lay epaulettes over shoulder seams, matching
cast-on edge to armhole edge, and sew
together at armhole edge. Secure other end in
place by attaching a button through both
layers.

Cuff trims (make 2)
Using 8mm (US 11) needles and yarn A cast
on 9 sts.
Work in rib as given for collar until cuff trim
meas 12 cm, ending with **WS** facing for next
row.
Cast off in rib (on **WS**).
Using photograph as a guide, sew cast-on edge
of cuff trim to WS of lower edge of cuff band
and fold cuff trim up onto RS of sleeve. Secure

in place by attaching a button through both
layers.
See information page for finishing instructions,
setting in sleeves using the set-in method.
Attach press fasteners to fasten front bands, and
button to right front end of hem band to
correspond with buttonhole.

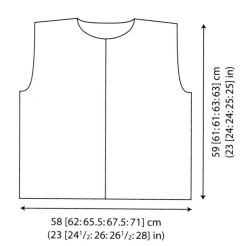

59 [61: 61: 63: 63] cm
(23 [24: 24: 25: 25] in)

58 [62: 65.5: 67.5: 71] cm
(23 [24$^{1}/_{2}$: 26: 26$^{1}/_{2}$: 28] in)

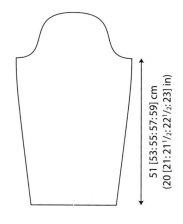

51 [53: 55: 57: 59] cm
(20 [21: 21$^{1}/_{2}$: 22$^{1}/_{2}$: 23] in)

BROGAN

by MARIE WALLIN

Main image page 3

YARN
Rowan Little Big Wool

A	Topaz 509	2 x 50gm
B	Amber 508	1 x 50gm
C	Amethyst 504	2 x 50gm
D	Quartz 506	2 x 50gm
E	Jasper 505	1 x 50gm
F	Onyx 501	1 x 50gm

NEEDLES
1 pair 8mm (no 0) (US 11) needles
1 pair 9mm (no 00) (US 13) needles

TENSION
13 sts and 14 rows to 10 cm measured over
patterned stocking stitch using 9mm (US 13)
needles.

LEGWARMERS (make 2)
Using 8mm (US 11) needles and yarn A cast
on 41 sts.
Row 1 (RS): K1, *P1, K1, rep from * to end.
Row 2: P1, *K1, P1, rep from * to end.
These 2 rows form rib.
Work in rib for a further 4 rows, dec 1 st at
end of last row and ending with RS facing
for next row. 40 sts.
Change to 9mm (US 13) needles.
Using the **fairisle** technique as described on
the information page, cont in patt from chart,
which is worked entirely in st st beg with a
K row, as folls:
Work 8 rows, ending with RS facing for
next row.
Inc 1 st at each end of next and every foll
6th row until there are 54 sts, taking inc sts
into patt.

44

Key ■ A ■ B ■ C □ D ■ E ■ F

Cont straight until chart row 79 has been completed, ending with **WS** facing for next row.
Change to 8mm (US 11) needles.
Break off all contrast and cont using yarn E **only**.
Next row (WS): Knit (to form fold line).

Beg with a K row, work in st st for 6 rows. Cast off.

MAKING UP
Press as described on the information page. Join back seam. Fold last 6 rows to inside along fold line row and slip stitch in place.

Using yarn A, make 2 twisted cords, each 65 cm long, and thread one cord through top casing of each legwarmer, beg and ending either side of back seam. Make four 4 cm diameter pompons, 2 in yarn B and 2 in yarn D, and attach pompons to ends of twisted cords as in photograph.

LILLITH
by MARIE WALLIN

Main image page 12 & 13

SIZE

8	10	12	14	16	18	
To fit bust						
82	87	92	97	102	107	cm
32	34	36	38	40	42	in

YARN
Rowan Little Big Wool

A Garnet 503

3	3	4	4	4	4	x 50gm

B Amethyst 504

2	2	2	3	3	3	x 50gm

C Jasper 505

2	2	2	2	2	2	x 50gm

D Onyx 501

3	3	3	3	3	3	x 50gm

NEEDLES
1 pair 8mm (no 0) (US 11) needles
1 pair 9mm (no 00) (US 13) needles

TENSION
11 sts and 15 rows to 10 cm measured over stocking stitch using 10mm (US 13) needles.

STRIPE SEQUENCE
Beg with a K row, work in st st in stripe sequence as folls:
Rows 1 to 6: Using yarn B.
Rows 7 and 8: Using yarn C.
Rows 9 to 12: Using yarn D.
Rows 13 to 18: Using yarn A.

Rows 19 to 22: Using yarn D.
Rows 23 to 26: Using yarn C.
Rows 27 and 28: Using yarn A.
Rows 29 and 30: Using yarn B.
Rows 31 and 32: Using yarn D.
Rows 33 and 34: Using yarn B.
Rows 35 to 40: Using yarn D.
Rows 41 to 46: Using yarn C.
Rows 47 to 50: Using yarn A.
Rows 51 and 52: Using yarn D.
Rows 53 and 54: Using yarn B.
Rows 55 and 56: Using yarn D.
Rows 57 to 60: Using yarn B.
Rows 61 and 62: Using yarn D.
Rows 63 to 66: Using yarn C.

Rows 67 and 68: Using yarn A.
Rows 69 and 70: Using yarn D.
Rows 71 and 72: Using yarn B.
Rows 73 and 74: Using yarn D.
Rows 75 to 78: Using yarn B.
Rows 79 and 80: Using yarn D.
Rows 81 to 84: Using yarn C.
Rows 85 and 86: Using yarn A.
These 86 rows form stripe sequence.

BACK
Using 8mm (US 11) needles and yarn A cast
on 46 [50: 50: 54: 58: 62] sts.
Row 1 (RS): K2, *P2, K2, rep from * to end.
Row 2: P2, *K2, P2, rep from * to end.
These 2 rows form rib.
Work in rib for a further 10 rows, inc [dec: inc:
inc: dec: dec] 1 st at end of last row and ending
with RS facing for next row.
47 [49: 51: 55: 57: 61] sts.
Change to 9mm (US 13) needles.
Beg with a K row, work in st st in stripe
sequence (see above) until back meas 31 [31:
30: 33: 32: 34] cm, ending with RS facing
for next row.
Shape armholes
Keeping stripes correct, cast off 3 sts at beg of
next 2 rows.
41 [43: 45: 49: 51: 55] sts.★★
Dec 1 st at each end of next 1 [1: 1: 3: 3: 3]
rows, then on foll 2 [2: 2: 2: 2: 3] alt rows.
35 [37: 39: 39: 41: 43] sts.
Cont straight until armhole meas 19 [19: 20:
20: 21: 21] cm, ending with RS facing for
next row.
Shape back neck
Next row (RS): K8 [9: 10: 10: 10: 11] and
turn, leaving rem sts on a holder.
Work each side of neck separately.
Cast off 3 sts at beg of next row.
5 [6: 7: 7: 7: 8] sts.
Work 2 rows, ending with RS facing for
next row.
Shape shoulder
Cast off rem 5 [6: 7: 7: 7: 8] sts.
With RS facing, rejoin appropriate yarn to rem
sts, cast off centre 19 [19: 19: 19: 21: 21] sts,
K to end.
Complete to match first side, reversing shapings.
FRONT
Work as given for back to ★★.
Shape neck
Next row (RS): K2tog, K14 [15: 16: 18:
18: 20] and turn, leaving rem sts on a holder.

Work each side of neck separately.
Dec 1 st at neck edge of next 4 rows, then on
foll 4 alt rows **and at same time** dec 1 st at
armhole edge of 2nd [2nd: 2nd: next: next:
next] and foll 0 [0: 0: 1: 1: 1] row, then on foll
1 [1: 1: 2: 2: 3] alt rows.
5 [6: 7: 7: 7: 8] sts.
Cont straight until front matches back to
shoulder cast-off, ending with RS facing for
next row.
Shape shoulder
Cast off rem 5 [6: 7: 7: 7: 8] sts.
With RS facing, rejoin appropriate yarn to rem
sts, cast off centre 9 [9: 9: 9: 11: 11] sts, K to last
2 sts, K2tog.
Complete to match first side, reversing shapings.

SLEEVES
Using 8mm (US 11) needles and yarn A cast
on 24 [24: 26: 26: 28: 28] sts.
Row 1 (RS): P1 [1: 0: 0: 0: 0], K2 [2: 0: 0:
1: 1], *P2, K2, rep from * to last 1 [1: 2: 2: 3: 3]
sts, P1 [1: 2: 2: 2: 2], K0 [0: 0: 0: 1: 1].
Row 2: K1 [1: 0: 0: 0: 0], P2 [2: 0: 0: 1: 1],
*K2, P2, rep from * to last 1 [1: 2: 2: 3: 3] sts,
K1 [1: 2: 2: 2: 2], P0 [0: 0: 0: 1: 1].
These 2 rows form rib.
Work in rib for a further 6 rows, ending with
RS facing for next row.
Change to 9mm (US 13) needles.
Beg with a K row and stripe row 65 [65: 61:
67: 63: 67], work in st st in stripe sequence (see
above), shaping sides by inc 1 st at each end of
5th and every foll 4th [4th: 4th: 4th: 6th: 6th]
row to 28 [28: 30: 30: 46: 46] sts, then on every
foll 6th [6th: 6th: 6th: –: –] row until there are
42 [42: 44: 44: –: –] sts.
Cont straight until sleeve meas approx 43 [43:
44: 44: 45: 45] cm, ending after same stripe row
as on back to beg of armhole shaping and with
RS facing for next row.
Shape top
Keeping stripes correct, cast off 3 sts at beg of
next 2 rows. 36 [36: 38: 38: 40: 40] sts.
Dec 1 st at each end of next 3 rows, then on
every foll alt row to 22 sts, then on foll 3 rows,
ending with RS facing for next row. 16 sts.
Cast off 4 sts at beg of next 2 rows.
Cast off rem 8 sts.

MAKING UP
Press as described on the information page.
Join right shoulder seam using back stitch, or
mattress stitch if preferred.

Neck band
With RS facing, using 8mm (US 11) needles
and yarn A, pick up and knit 28 [28: 30: 30:
30: 30] sts down left side of front neck, 9 [9: 9:
9: 11: 11] sts from front, 28 [28: 30: 30: 30: 30]
sts up right side of front neck, 3 sts down right
side of back neck, 19 [19: 19: 19: 21: 21] sts
from back, then 3 sts up left side of back neck.
90 [90: 94: 94: 98: 98] sts.
Beg with row 2, work in rib as given for
back for 4 rows, ending with WS facing for
next row.
Cast off in rib (on **WS**).
See information page for finishing instructions,
setting in sleeves using the set-in method.

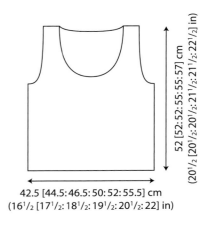

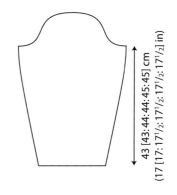

JOCELYN

by MARIE WALLIN

Main image page 9

YARN

Rowan Little Big Wool

A	Jasper 505	4 x 50gm
B	Amethyst 504	1 x 50gm
C	Onyx 501	2 x 50gm
D	Amber 508	2 x 50gm
E	Topaz 509	1 x 50gm
F	Garnet 503	2 x 50gm

NEEDLES

1 pair 8mm (no 0) (US 11) needles
1 pair 9mm (no 00) (US 13) needles

TENSION

13 sts and 14 rows to 10 cm measured over patterned stocking stitch using 9mm (US 13) needles.

FINISHED SIZE

Completed scarf measures 53 cm (21 in) wide and 145 cm (57 in) long, excluding fringe.

Pattern note: The chart patt rep is an odd number of rows. On the first and 3rd rep, work odd numbered rows as **WS purl** rows reading chart from left to right. On the 2nd and 4th rep, work odd numbered rows as RS knit rows reading chart from right to left.

SCARF

Using 8mm (US 11) needles and yarn A cast on 67 sts.
Work in g st for 5 rows, ending with **WS** facing for next row.
Change to 9mm (US 13) needles.
Beg and ending rows as indicated, using the

fairisle technique as described on the information page and repeating the 49 row patt repeat throughout, cont in patt from chart, which is worked entirely in st st beg with a K row, as folls:
Work 196 rows, ending after 4th rep of chart row 49 and with **WS** facing for next row.
Change to 8mm (US 11) needles.
Using yarn A, work in g st for 4 rows, ending with **WS** facing for next row.
Cast off knitwise (on **WS**).

MAKING UP

Press as described on the information page.
Side borders (both alike)
With RS facing, using 8mm (US 11) needles and yarn A, pick up and knit 182 sts along one row-end edge, between cast-on and cast-off edges.
Cast off knitwise (on **WS**).
Cut 72 lengths of yarn A, each 35 cm long, and knot groups of 6 of these lengths through cast-on and cast-off edge of scarf, placing 6 evenly spaced knots along each end.

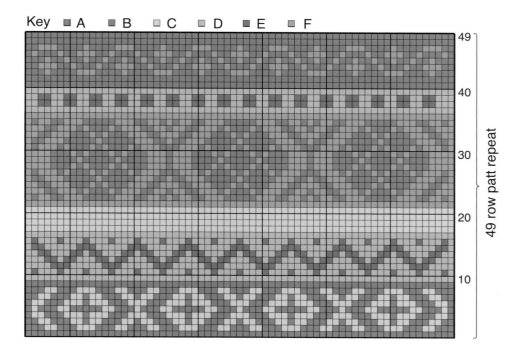

FALLON

by MARIE WALLIN

Main image page 17

SIZE

8	10	12	14	16	18	
To fit bust						
82	87	92	97	102	107	cm
32	34	36	38	40	42	in

YARN

Rowan Big Wool Fusion

5	6	6	7	7	8	x 100gm

(photographed in Smokey 007)

NEEDLES

1 pair 10mm (no 000) (US 15) needles

BUTTONS – 4 x 00406

TENSION

10 sts and 18 rows to 10 cm measured over garter stitch using 10mm (US 15) needles.

BACK

Using 10mm (US 15) needles cast on 38 [40: 42: 46: 48: 52] sts.
Work in g st, shaping side seams by inc 1 st at each end of 9th and foll 10th row.
42 [44: 46: 50: 52: 56] sts.
Cont straight until back meas 16 [16: 15: 18: 17: 19] cm, ending with RS facing for next row.

Shape armholes

Place markers at both ends of last row to denote base of armholes.
Dec 1 st at each end of next 1 [2: 3: 4: 4: 5] rows.
40 [40: 40: 42: 44: 46] sts.
Cont straight until armhole meas 21 [21: 22: 22: 23: 23] cm, ending with RS facing for

next row.

Shape shoulders

Cast off all sts, placing markers either side of centre 24 [24: 24: 24: 26: 26] sts to denote back neck.

LEFT FRONT

Using 10mm (US 15) needles cast on 21 [22: 23: 25: 26: 28] sts.
Work in g st, shaping side seam by inc 1 st at beg of 9th and foll 10th row.
23 [24: 25: 27: 28: 30] sts.
Cont straight until left front matches back to beg of armhole shaping, ending with RS facing for next row.

Shape armhole and front slope

Place marker at end of last row to denote base of armhole.
Next row (RS): K2tog, K to last 3 sts, K2tog, K1.
Working all front slope shaping as set by last row, dec 1 st at front slope edge of 2nd and foll 9 [9: 8: 8: 9: 9] alt rows, then on 3 [3: 4: 4: 4: 4] foll 4th rows **and at same time** dec 1 st at armhole edge of next 0 [1: 2: 3: 3: 4] rows.
8 [8: 8: 9: 9: 10] sts.
Cont straight until left front matches back to shoulder cast-off, ending with RS facing for next row.

Shape shoulder

Cast off.
Mark positions for 4 buttons along left front opening edge – first to come in row 3, last to come just below beg of front slope shaping, and rem 2 buttons evenly spaced between.

RIGHT FRONT

Using 10mm (US 15) needles cast on 21 [22: 23: 25: 26: 28] sts.
Work in g st for 2 rows, ending with RS facing for next row.
Row 3 (buttonhole row) (RS): K1, K2tog, yfwd, K to end.
Working a further 3 buttonholes in this way to correspond to positions marked for buttons, cont in g st, shaping side seam by inc 1 st at end of 6th and foll 10th row.
23 [24: 25: 27: 28: 30] sts.
Cont straight until right front matches back to beg of armhole shaping, ending with RS facing for next row.

Shape armhole and front slope

Place marker at beg of last row to denote base of armhole.
Next row (RS): K1, K2tog, K to last 2 sts, K2tog.
Working all front slope shaping as set by last row, complete to match left front, reversing shapings.

SLEEVES

Using 10mm (US 15) needles cast on 24 [24: 26: 26: 26: 26] sts.
Work in g st, shaping sides by inc 1 st at each end of 7th [7th: 9th: 9th: 7th: 7th] and every foll 10th [10th: 10th: 10th: 8th: 8th] row to 38 [38: 40: 40: 34: 34] sts, then on every foll – [–: –: –: 10th: 10th] row until there are – [–: –: –: 42: 42] sts.
Cont straight until sleeve meas 43 [43: 44: 44: 45: 45] cm, ending with RS facing for next row.

Shape top

Place markers at both ends of last row to denote top of sleeve seam.

Dec 1 st at each end of next 1 [2: 3: 4: 4: 5] rows.
Work 1 [0: 1: 0: 0: 1] row, ending with RS facing for next row.
Cast off rem 36 [34: 34: 32: 34: 32] sts.

MAKING UP
Press as described on the information page.
Join both shoulder seams using back stitch, or mattress stitch if preferred.
See information page for finishing instructions, setting in sleeves using the shallow set-in method.

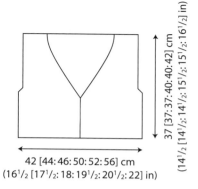

42 [44: 46: 50: 52: 56] cm
(16¹/₂ [17¹/₂: 18: 19¹/₂: 20¹/₂: 22] in)

37 [37: 37: 40: 40: 42] cm
(14¹/₂ [14¹/₂: 14¹/₂: 15¹/₂: 15¹/₂: 16¹/₂] in)

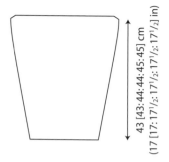

43 [43: 44: 44: 45: 45] cm
(17 [17: 17¹/₂: 17¹/₂: 17¹/₂: 17¹/₂] in)

LARISSA

by MARIE WALLIN

Main image page 16

SIZE

8	10	12	14	16	18	20	22	

To fit bust

82	87	92	97	102	107	112	117	cm
32	34	36	38	40	42	44	46	in

YARN
Rowan Little Big Wool

9	9	10	11	11	12	12	13	x 50gm

(photographed in Amethyst 504)

NEEDLES
1 pair 9mm (no 00) (US 13) needles
8mm (no 0) (US 11) circular needle

8.00mm (no 0) (US L11) crochet hook

TENSION
11 sts and 15 rows to 10 cm measured over stocking stitch using 9mm (US 13) needles.

UK CROCHET ABBREVIATIONS
ch = chain; **dc** = double crochet;
ss = slip stitch.

US CROCHET ABBREVIATIONS
ch = chain; **dc** = single crochet;
ss = slip stitch.

BACK
Using 9mm (US 13) needles cast on 47 [49: 51: 55: 57: 61: 65: 67] sts.
Beg with a K row, work in st st for 20 rows.
Dec 1 st at each end of next row.
45 [47: 49: 53: 55: 59: 63: 65] sts.
Work 9 rows, ending with RS facing for next row.
Inc 1 st at each end of next row.
47 [49: 51: 55: 57: 61: 65: 67] sts.
Cont straight until back meas 30 [30: 29: 32: 31: 33: 32: 34] cm, ending with RS facing for next row.

Shape armholes

Cast off 2 sts at beg of next 2 rows.
43 [45: 47: 51: 53: 57: 61: 63] sts.
Dec 1 st at each end of next 3 [3: 3: 3: 3: 5: 5: 5] rows, then on foll 0 [0: 0: 2: 2: 1: 2: 2] alt rows.
37 [39: 41: 41: 43: 45: 47: 49] sts.
Cont straight until armhole meas 20 [20: 21: 21: 22: 22: 23: 23] cm, ending with RS facing for next row.

Shape shoulders and back neck

Next row (RS): Cast off 3 [4: 4: 4: 4: 5: 5: 6] sts, K until there are 7 [7: 8: 8: 8: 8: 9: 9] sts on right needle and turn, leaving rem sts on a holder.
Work each side of neck separately.
Cast off 3 sts at beg of next row.
Cast off rem 4 [4: 5: 5: 5: 5: 6: 6] sts.
With RS facing, rejoin yarn to rem sts, cast off centre 17 [17: 17: 17: 19: 19: 19: 19] sts, K to end.
Complete to match first side, reversing shapings.

LEFT FRONT

Using 9mm (US 13) needles cast on 22 [23: 24: 26: 27: 29: 31: 32] sts.
Beg with a K row, work in st st for 20 rows.
Dec 1 st at beg of next row.
21 [22: 23: 25: 26: 28: 30: 31] sts.
Work 9 rows, ending with RS facing for next row.
Inc 1 st at beg of next row.
22 [23: 24: 26: 27: 29: 31: 32] sts.
Cont straight until 6 rows less have been worked than on back to beg of armhole shaping, ending with RS facing for next row.

Shape front slope

Dec 1 st at end of next and foll 2 alt rows.
19 [20: 21: 23: 24: 26: 28: 29] sts.
Work 1 row, ending with RS facing for next row.

Shape armhole

Cast off 2 sts at beg and dec 1 [1: 0: 0: 1: 1: 1: 1] st at end of next row.
16 [17: 19: 21: 21: 23: 25: 26] sts.
Work 1 row.
Dec 1 st at armhole edge of next 3 [3: 3: 3: 3: 5: 5: 5] rows, then on foll 0 [0: 0: 2: 2: 1: 2: 2] alt rows **and at same time** dec 1 st at front slope edge of 3rd [3rd: next: next: 3rd: 3rd: 3rd: 3rd] and foll 0 [0: 0: 4th: 4th: 4th: 4th: 4th] row.
12 [13: 15: 14: 14: 15: 16: 17] sts.
Dec 1 st at front slope edge **only** of 4th [4th: 2nd: 2nd: 4th: 4th: 2nd: 2nd] and every foll 4th row until 7 [8: 9: 9: 9: 10: 11: 12] sts rem.
Cont straight until left front matches back to beg of shoulder shaping, ending with RS

facing for next row.

Shape shoulder

Cast off 3 [4: 4: 4: 4: 5: 5: 6] sts at beg of next row.
Work 1 row.
Cast off rem 4 [4: 5: 5: 5: 5: 6: 6] sts.

RIGHT FRONT

Using 9mm (US 13) needles cast on 22 [23: 24: 26: 27: 29: 31: 32] sts.
Beg with a K row, work in st st for 20 rows.
Dec 1 st at end of next row.
21 [22: 23: 25: 26: 28: 30: 31] sts.
Complete to match left front, reversing shapings.

SLEEVES

Using 9mm (US 13) needles cast on 28 [28: 30: 30: 32: 32: 34: 34] sts.
Beg with a K row, work in st st, shaping sides by inc 1 st at each end of 7th and every foll 8th row to 40 [40: 42: 42: 42: 42: 46: 46] sts, then on every foll 10th row until there are 42 [42: 44: 44: 46: 46: 48: 48] sts.
Cont straight until sleeve meas 43 [43: 44: 45: 45: 44: 44] cm, ending with RS facing for next row.

Shape top

Cast off 2 sts at beg of next 2 rows. 38 [38: 40: 40: 42: 42: 44: 44] sts.
Dec 1 st at each end of next 7 rows, then on foll 0 [0: 1: 1: 2: 2: 3: 3] alt rows, then on foll 5 rows, ending with RS facing for next row. 14 sts.
Cast off 4 sts at beg of next 2 rows.
Cast off rem 6 sts.

MAKING UP

Press as described on the information page.
Join both shoulder seams using back stitch, or mattress stitch if preferred.

Front band

With RS facing and using 8mm (US 11) circular needle, beg and ending at cast-on edges, pick up and knit 39 [39: 38: 41: 40: 42: 41: 43] sts up right front opening edge to beg of front slope shaping, 34 [34: 35: 35: 36: 36: 37: 37] sts up right front slope, 31 [31: 31: 31: 33: 33: 33: 33] sts from back, 34 [34: 35: 35: 36: 36: 37: 37] sts down left front slope to beg of front slope shaping, then 39 [39: 38: 41: 40: 42: 41: 43] sts down left front opening edge.
177 [177: 177: 183: 185: 189: 189: 193] sts.
Row 1 (WS): Purl.
Row 2: Inc knitwise in first st, *inc purlwise in next st, inc knitwise in next st, rep from * to end. 354 [354: 354: 366: 370: 378: 378: 386] sts.
Change to 9mm (US 13) circular needle.
Row 3: P2, *K2, P2, rep from * to end.
Row 4: K2, *P2, K2, rep from * to end.

Rep last 2 rows 3 times more, ending with WS facing for next row.
Cast off in rib.
See information page for finishing instructions, setting in sleeves using the set-in method.

Hem edging

With RS facing and using 8.00mm (US L11) crochet hook, attach yarn to base of front band pick-up row of left front, 1 ch (does NOT count as st), now working into each st around cast-on edge cont as folls: 1 dc into first st, *3 ch, 1 dc into next st, rep from * to end.
Fasten off.

Cuff edging

With RS facing and using 8.00mm (US L11) crochet hook, attach yarn to base of sleeve seam, 1 ch (does NOT count as st), now working into each st around cast-on edge cont as folls: 1 dc into first st, *3 ch, 1 dc into next st, rep from * to end, replacing dc at end of last rep with ss to first dc.
Fasten off.
Make two 35 cm long twisted cords and knot one end to form a tiny tassel. Attach other end of each cord to inside of front band pick-up row level with beg of front slope shaping.

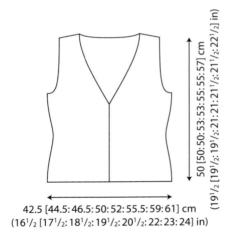

50 [50: 50: 53: 53: 55: 55: 57] cm
(19¹/₂ [19¹/₂: 19¹/₂: 21: 21: 21¹/₂: 21¹/₂: 22¹/₂] in)

42.5 [44.5: 46.5: 50: 52: 55.5: 59: 61] cm
(16¹/₂ [17¹/₂: 18¹/₂: 19¹/₂: 20¹/₂: 22: 23: 24] in)

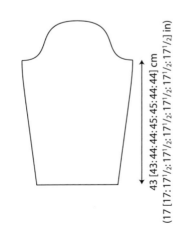

43 [43: 44: 44: 45: 45: 44: 44] cm
(17 [17: 17¹/₂: 17¹/₂: 17¹/₂: 17¹/₂: 17¹/₂: 17¹/₂] in)

RAPHAEL

by MARIE WALLIN

Main image page 19

SIZE

	S-M	L	XL-XXL	
To fit chest				
	102-107	112	117-122	cm
	40-42	44	46-48	in

YARN

Rowan Biggy Print

| | 21 | 24 | 27 | x 100gm |

(photographed in Shadow 265)

NEEDLES

1 pair 10mm (no 000) (US 15) needles
1 pair 12mm (US 17) needles

ZIP – open-ended zip to fit

TENSION

7 sts and 10 rows to 10 cm measured over stocking stitch using 12mm (US 17) needles.

BACK

Using 10mm (US 15) needles cast on 44 [50: 56] sts.
Beg with a K row, work in st st for 6 rows, ending with RS facing for next row.
Change to 12mm (US 17) needles.
Cont in st st until back meas 42 [41: 39] cm, ending with RS facing for next row.
Shape armholes
Cast off 5 [6: 7] sts at beg of next 2 rows.
34 [38: 42] sts.
Cont straight until armhole meas 25 [26: 28] cm, ending with RS facing for next row.
Shape shoulders and back neck
Next row (RS): Cast off 5 [5: 6] sts, K until there are 8 [9: 9] sts on right needle and turn,

leaving rem sts on a holder.
Work each side of neck separately.
Cast off 3 sts at beg of next row.
Cast off rem 5 [6: 6] sts.
With RS facing, rejoin yarn to rem sts, cast off centre 8 [10: 12] sts, K to end.
Complete to match first side, reversing shapings.

BLOCK A (make 13)

Using 12mm (US 17) needles cast on 10 [11: 12] sts.
Row 1 (WS): Knit.
Row 2: (K1, P1) 5 [5: 6] times, K0 [1: 0].
Rep last 2 rows 5 times more.
Cast off.

HALF BLOCK A (make 3)

Using 12mm (US 17) needles cast on 6 [7: 8] sts.
Row 1 (WS): Knit.
Row 2: (K1, P1) 3 [3: 4] times, K0 [1: 0].
Rep last 2 rows 5 times more.
Cast off.

QUARTER BLOCK A (make 1)

Using 12mm (US 17) needles cast on 6 [7: 8] sts.
Row 1 (WS): Knit.
Row 2: (K1, P1) 3 [3: 4] times, K0 [1: 0].
Rep last 2 rows 2 [1: 0] times more.
Cast off.

BLOCK B (make 13)

Using 12mm (US 17) needles cast on 10 [11: 12] sts.

Beg with a K row, work in st st for 12 rows, ending with RS facing for next row.
Cast off.

HALF BLOCK B (make 3)

Using 12mm (US 17) needles cast on

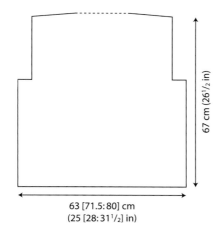

67 cm (26½ in)

63 [71.5: 80] cm
(25 [28: 31½] in)

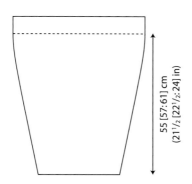

55 [57: 61] cm
(21½ [22½: 24] in)

6 [7: 8] sts.
Beg with a K row, work in st st for 12 rows, ending with RS facing for next row.
Cast off.

QUARTER BLOCK B (make 1)
Using 12mm (US 17) needles cast on 6 [7: 8] sts.
Beg with a K row, work in st st for 6 [4: 2] rows, ending with RS facing for next row.
Cast off.

SLEEVES
Using 10mm (US 15) needles cast on

22 [22: 24] sts.
Beg with a K row, work in st st for 6 rows, ending with RS facing for next row.
Change to 12mm (US 17) needles.
Cont in st st, shaping sides by inc 1 st at each end of next and every foll 6th row to 28 [34: 32] sts, then on every foll 8th row until there are 36 [38: 40] sts.
Cont straight until sleeve meas 62 [65: 71] cm, ending with RS facing for next row.
Cast off.

MAKING UP
Press as described on the information page.

Using diagram as a guide, sew blocks together to form left and right fronts – join pieces with **WS** together so that seams show on RS.
Back collar
With RS facing and using 10mm (US 15) needles, pick up and knit 14 [16: 18] sts from back neck.
Beg with a P row, work in st st for 11 rows, ending with RS facing for next row.
Cast off.
Join both shoulder and collar seams using back stitch, or mattress stitch if preferred.
See information page for finishing instructions, setting in sleeves using the square set-in method.

NOTES

CROCHET STITCHES

Although the crochet effects used within these designs may seem daunting to the beginner, they are actually very simple and use the very basic crochet stitches.

We hope this article will explain the basic stitches needed to complete the designs within Arabesque, and encourage everyone to pick up a crochet hook and 'have a go'. You will be surprised how easy it is and once you have mastered the basics, you can then go onto create some beautiful effects.

MAKING A CHAIN STITCH (CH) AND FOUNDATION CHAIN.

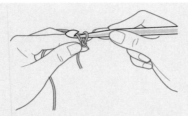
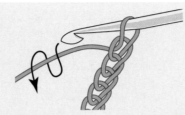

1. All crochet is started by making a slip knot in exactly the same way as you would begin knitting. Slip this knot onto the crochet hook and you're ready to make your first foundation chain. As when knitting, this slip knot is your first stitch.

2. Hold the crochet hook in your right hand

and grip the base of the slip knot between the thumb and first finger of the left hand. Wind the ball end of the yarn (working) around the fingers of your left hand to control the tension – exactly as you would when knitting but on the other hand. To make the first **chain**, twist the hook back and under the working strand of yarn so

that it loops around the hook. Pull this new loop of yarn through the loop already on the hook and you have made another chain.

3. Continue in this way, drawing new loops of yarn through the loop on the hook, until you have made the required number of chains.

MAKING A SLIP STITCH (SS).

1. A **slip stitch** is the very shortest and easiest of the basic stitches. To work a slip stitch, insert the hook into the work and take the yarn over the hook in the same

way as if you were going to make a chain stitch. Pull this new loop of yarn through both the work and the loop on the hook – this completes the slip stitch.

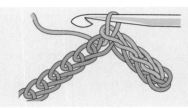

MAKING A DOUBLE CROCHET (DC) AMERICAN SINGLE CROCHET (SC)

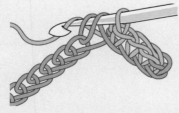
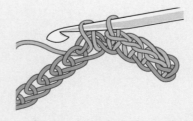

1. The next tallest stitch, the **double crochet** is one of the two most commonly used crochet stitches. This is worked in a similar way to a slip stitch. Start by inserting the hook into the work, and taking the yarn over the hook.

2. Draw this new loop through just the work, leaving two loops on the hook.

3. Take the yarn over the hook again. Draw this new loop through both the loops on the hook thereby completing the double crochet stitch.

MAKING A TREBLE (TR) AMERICAN DOUBLE CROCHET (DC)

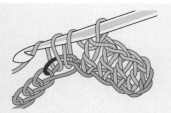
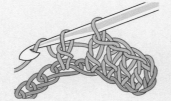
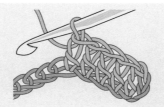
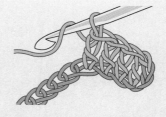

1. The other most commonly used crochet stitch is the **treble**. To make a treble start by taking the yarn over the hook BEFORE inserting into the work.

2. Then insert the hook into the work, take

the yarn over the hook again and draw this new loop through. There are now three loops on the hook.

3. Take the yarn over the hook and draw this new loop through the first two loops only

on the hook. There are now two loops on the hook.

4. Take the yarn over the hook, and draw this through the remaining two loops on the hook to complete the treble stitch.

MAKING A DOUBLE TREBLE (DTR) AMERICAN TREBLE (TR)

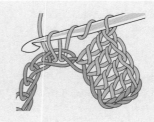

1. The taller **double treble** is worked as for the treble, except that the yarn is wrapped around the hook twice before it is inserted into the work. To begin take the yarn twice round the hook. Insert the hook into the work, take the yarn over the hook and draw through the work. There are now four loops on the hook. Take the yarn over the

hook and draw through the first two loops only on the hook. There are now three loops on the hook. Continue taking the yarn over the hook and drawing through two loops at a time until just one loop remains. The double treble is now complete.

WORKING IN ROUNDS.

1. To start a piece of circular crochet, begin by making the foundation chain. Now secure the ends of this chain to each other by working a slip stitch into the first chain to form a loop.

2. Make sure you don't twist the chain before you join the ends as this could make the work

twisted or the stitches uneven. The first 'round' of crochet is worked into the ring. The instructions in the pattern will tell you which stitches and how many need to be worked.

3. At the end of each round you will need to secure the last stitch to the first stitch to close

the round. Do this by working a slip stitch into the top of the first stitch. Also in following rounds the stitches need to be raised, this is done by working twice into the same stitch were instructed. The work is not turned at the end of a round, so the right side is always facing you.

FASTENING OFF.

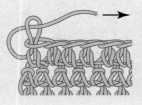

To fasten off your crochet work, cut the yarn about 8cm from the work. Pass this loose end through the one remaining loop

on the hook and pull tight. Darn the loose ends into the back of the work, using a blunt ended needle.

INFORMATION

TENSION

Obtaining the correct tension is perhaps the single factor which can make the difference between a successful garment and a disastrous one. It controls both the shape and size of an article, so any variation, however slight, can distort the finished garment. Different designers feature in our books and it is **their** tension, given at the **start** of each pattern, which you must match. We recommend that you knit a square in pattern and/or stocking stitch (depending on the pattern instructions) of perhaps 5 - 10 more stitches and 5 - 10 more rows than those given in the tension note. Mark out the central 10cm square with pins. If you have too many stitches to 10cm try again using thicker needles, if you have too few stitches to 10cm try again using finer needles. Once you have achieved the correct tension your garment will be knitted to the measurements indicated in the size diagram shown at the end of the pattern.

SIZING & SIZE DIAGRAM NOTE

The instructions are given for the smallest size. Where they vary, work the figures in brackets for the larger sizes. **One set of figures refers to all sizes.** Included with most patterns in this brochure is a **'size diagram'**, or sketch of the finished garment and its dimensions. The size diagram shows the finished width of the garment at the under-arm point, and it is this measurement that the knitter should choose first; a useful tip is to measure one of your own garments which is a comfortable fit. Having chosen a size based on width, look at the corresponding length for that size; if you are not happy with the total length which we recommend, adjust your own garment before beginning your armhole shaping - any adjustment after this point will mean that your sleeve will not fit into your garment easily - don't forget to take your adjustment into account if there is any side seam shaping. Finally, look at the sleeve length; the size diagram shows the finished sleeve measurement, taking into account any top-arm insertion length. Measure your body between the centre of your neck and your wrist, this measurement should correspond to half the garment width plus the sleeve length. Again, your sleeve length may be adjusted, but remember to take into consideration your sleeve increases if you do

adjust the length - you must increase more frequently than the pattern states to shorten your sleeve, less frequently to lengthen it.

CHART NOTE

Many of the patterns in the brochure are worked from charts. Each square on a chart represents a stitch and each line of squares a row of knitting. Each colour used is given a different letter and these are shown in the **materials** section, or in the **key** alongside the chart of each pattern. When working from the charts, read odd rows (K) from right to left and even rows (P) from left to right, unless otherwise stated.

KNITTING WITH COLOUR

There are two main methods of working colour into a knitted fabric: **Intarsia** and **Fairisle** techniques. The first method produces a single thickness of fabric and is usually used where a colour is only required in a particular area of a row and does not form a repeating pattern across the row, as in the fairisle technique.

Intarsia: The simplest way to do this is to cut short lengths of yarn for each motif or block of colour used in a row. Then joining in the various colours at the appropriate point on the row, link one colour to the next by twisting them around each other where they meet on the wrong side to avoid gaps. All ends can then either be darned along the colour join lines, as each motif is completed or then can be " knitted-in" to the fabric of the knitting as each colour is worked into the pattern. This is done in much the same way as "weaving- in" yarns when working the Fairisle technique and does save time darning-in ends. It is essential that the tension is noted for **Intarsia** as this may vary from the stocking stitch if both are used in the same pattern.

Fairisle type knitting: When two or three colours are worked repeatedly across a row, strand the yarn **not** in use loosely behind the stitches being worked. If you are working with more than two colours, treat the "floating" yarns as if they were one yarn and always spread the stitches to their correct width to keep them elastic. It is advisable not to carry the stranded or "floating" yarns over more than three stitches at a time, but to weave them under and over

the colour you are working. The "floating" yarns are therefore caught at the back of the work.

FINISHING INSTRUCTIONS

After working for hours knitting a garment, it seems a great pity that many garments are spoiled because such little care is taken in the pressing and finishing process. Follow the following tips for a truly professional-looking garment.

PRESSING

Block out each piece of knitting and following the instructions on the ball band press the garment pieces, omitting the ribs. Tip: Take special care to press the edges, as this will make sewing up both easier and neater. If the ball band indicates that the fabric is not to be pressed, then covering the blocked out fabric with a damp white cotton cloth and leaving it to stand will have the desired effect. Darn in all ends neatly along the selvage edge or a colour join, as appropriate.

STITCHING

When stitching the pieces together, remember to match areas of colour and texture very carefully where they meet. Use a seam stitch such as back stitch or mattress stitch for all main knitting seams and join all ribs and neckband with mattress stitch, unless otherwise stated.

CONSTRUCTION

Having completed the pattern instructions, join left shoulder and neckband seams as detailed above. Sew the top of the sleeve to the body of the garment using the method detailed in the pattern, referring to the appropriate guide:

Shallow set-in sleeves: Match decreases at beg of armhole shaping to decreases at top of sleeve. Sew sleeve head into armhole, easing in shapings.

Set- in sleeves: Place centre of cast-off edge of sleeve to shoulder seam. Set in sleeve, easing sleeve head into armhole.

Join side and sleeve seams.
Slip stitch pocket edgings and linings into place.
Sew on buttons to correspond with buttonholes.
Ribbed welts and neckbands and any areas of garter stitch should not be pressed.

ABBREVIATIONS & EXPERIENCE RATINGS

K	knit	**cm**	centimetres	
P	purl	**in(s)**	inch(es)	
st(s)	stitch(es)	**RS**	right side	
inc	increas(e)(ing)	**WS**	wrong side	
dec	decreas(e)(ing)	**sl 1**	slip one stitch	
st st	stocking stitch (1 row K, 1 row P)	**psso**	pass slipped stitch over	
g st	garter stitch (K every row)	**tbl**	through back of loop	
beg	begin(ning)	**yrn**	yarn round needle	
foll	following	**yfwd**	yarn forward	
rem	remain(ing)	**meas**	measures	
rev st st	reverse stocking stitch (1 row P, 1 row K)	**0**	no stitches, times or rows	
rep	repeat	**–**	no stitches, times or rows for that size	
alt	alternate	**approx**	approximately	
cont	continue	**m1**	make one stitch by picking up horizontal loop before next stitch and knitting into back of it	
patt	pattern			
tog	together			
mm	millimetres			

Easy, straight forward knitting / crocheting

Suitable for the average knitter / crocheter

For the more experienced knitter

STOCKISTS

AUSTRALIA:
Australian Country Spinners,
314 Albert Street, Brunswick,
Victoria 3056
Tel: (61) 3 9380 3888 Fax: (61) 3 9387 2674
E-mail: sales@auspinners.com.au

BELGIUM:
Pavan,
Meerlaanstraat 73, B9860 Balegem (Oosterzele).
Tel: (32) 9 221 8594   Fax: (32) 9 221 8594
E-mail: pavan@pandora.be

CANADA:
Diamond Yarn,
9697 St Laurent, Montreal, Quebec, H3L 2N1
Tel: (514) 388 6188

Diamond Yarn (Toronto),
155 Martin Ross, Unit 3, Toronto, Ontario, M3J 2L9
Tel: (416) 736 6111   Fax: (416) 736 6112
E-mail: diamond@diamondyarn.com
www.diamondyarn.com

DENMARK:
Coats Danmark A/S, Mariendlunds Alle 4,
7430 Ikast
Tel: (45) 96 60 34 00   Fax: (45) 96 60 34 08
Email: coats@coats.dk

FINLAND:
Coats Opti Oy,
Ketjutie 3, 04220 Kerava
Tel: (358) 9 274 871 Fax: (358) 9 2748 7330
E-mail: coatsopti.sales@coats.com

FRANCE:
Coats France / Steiner Frères,
100, avenue du Général de Gaulle,
18 500 Mehun-Sur-Yèvre
Tel: (33) 02 48 23 12 30   Fax: (33) 02 48 23 12 40

GERMANY:
Coats GMbH,
Kaiserstrasse 1, D-79341 Kenzingen
Tel: (49) 7644 8020   Fax: (49) 7644 802399.
www.coatsgmbh.de

HOLLAND:
de Afstap,
Oude Leliestraat 12, 1015 AW Amsterdam
Tel: (31) 20 6231445 Fax: (31) 20 427 8522

HONG KONG:
East Unity Co Ltd,
Unit B2, 7/F Block B, Kailey Industrial Centre,
12 Fung Yip Street, Chai Wan
Tel: (852) 2869 7110 Fax: (852) 2537 6952
E-mail: eastuni@netvigator.com

ICELAND:
Storkurinn, Laugavegi 59, 101 Reykjavik
Tel: (354) 551 8258
Fax: (354) 562 8252
E-mail: malin@mmedia.is

ITALY: D.L.
srl, Via Piave,
24 – 26, 20016 Pero, Milan
Tel: (39) 02 339 10 180   Fax: (39) 02 33914661

JAPAN:
Puppy Co Ltd,
T151-0051, 3-16-5 Sendagaya, Shibuyaku, Tokyo
Tel: (81) 3 3490 2827 Fax: (81) 3 5412 7738
E-mail: info@rowan-jaeger.com

KOREA:
Coats Korea Co Ltd,
5F Kuckdong B/D, 935-40 Bangbae- Dong,
Seocho-Gu, Seoul
Tel: (82) 2 521 6262. Fax: (82) 2 521 5181

NEW ZEALAND:
Please contact Rowan for details of stockists

NORWAY:
Coats Knappehuset AS,
Pb 100 Ulste, 5873 Bergen
Tel: (47) 55 53 93 00   Fax: (47) 55 53 93 93

SINGAPORE:
Golden Dragon Store,
101 Upper Cross Street #02-51, People's Park
Centre, Singapore 058357
Tel: (65) 6 5358454 Fax : (65) 6 2216278
E-mail: gdscraft@hotmail.com

SOUTH AFRICA:
Arthur Bales PTY,
PO Box 44644, Linden 2104
Tel: (27) 11 888 2401 Fax: (27) 11 782 6137

SPAIN:
Oyambre,
Pau Claris 145, 80009 Barcelona.
Tel: (34) 670 011957   Fax: (34) 93 4872672
E-mail: oyambre@oyambreonline.com

SWEDEN:
Coats Expotex AB,
Division Craft, Box 297, 401 24 Grteborg
Tel: (46) 33 720 79 00 Fax: 46 31 47 16 50

TAIWAN:
Laiter Wool Knitting Co Ltd,
10-1 313 Lane, Sec 3, Chung Ching North Road,
Taipei
Tel: (886) 2 2596 0269 Fax : (886) 2 2598 0619

Mon Cher Corporation,
9F No 117 Chung Sun First Road, Kaoshiung
Tel: (886) 7 9711988   Fax: (886) 7 9711666

U.S.A.:
Westminster Fibers Inc,
4 Townsend West, Suite 8, Nashua,
New Hampshire 03063
Tel: (1 603) 886 5041 / 5043 Fax (1 603) 886 1056
E-mail: rowan@westminsterfibers.com

U.K:
Rowan,
Green Lane Mill, Holmfirth, West Yorkshire,
England HD9 2DX
Tel: +44 (0) 1484 681881 Fax: +44 (0) 1484 687920
E-mail: mail@knitrowan.com
Inernet: www.knitrowan.com

**For stockists in all other countries please
contact Rowan for stockist details.**